HARVARD EAST ASIAN SERIES, 3

The East Asian Research Center at Harvard University administers postgraduate training programs and research projects designed to further scholarly understanding of China, Korea, Japan, and adjacent areas.

REFORM
IN SUNG CHINA

REFORM
IN SUNG CHINA

Wang An-shih (1021–1086) and his New Policies

James T. C. Liu

Harvard University Press
Cambridge, Massachusetts

© 1959, by the President and Fellows of Harvard College
Second Printing, 1968
Distributed in Great Britain by Oxford University Press, London

Preparation of this volume was aided by a grant from the Carnegie
Corporation. The Corporation is not, however, the author, owner,
publisher, or proprietor of this publication and is not to be understood as approving by virtue of its grant any of the statements
made or views expressed therein.

Publication has been aided by a grant
from the Ford Foundation.

Library of Congress Catalog Card Number 59–9281

Printed in the United States of America

To my father Liu Shih-sun
(1886–1957)

Foreword

Professor James T. C. Liu's new appraisal of Wang An-shih and his times is an interdisciplinary study which builds upon recent scholarship and at the same time presents an individual view of the subject. It is interdisciplinary because it combines approaches and techniques of analysis drawn from political science, history, and sinology. The author's careful use of materials meets the high standards of critical humanistic study; his interest in interpretation reveals a keen sense of problem such as is necessary for any political scientist. The resulting volume serves a dual purpose: it draws upon the numerous specific researches of modern Chinese and Japanese scholars, which are helpful to the understanding of aspects of the subject, and it prepares the ground for an exhaustive and definitive work, which of course will take a much longer time to accomplish. By consolidating the relevant results from these individual researches and from his own studies, Professor Liu is in a position to explore new angles of investigation and to stimulate further research.

The problems dealt with in this volume include issues in political thought, the behavior patterns of Chinese bureaucrats, and questions related to the centralization of state power. The significance of these topics will be readily admitted by all students of institutions and of intellectual history. In preparing this volume the author has taken care not to burden his readers with unnecessary details or special jargon. On the other hand, he does not shun complicated problems simply because they are difficult to explain.

For this reason, Professor Liu's choice of "Service for Local Government," to serve as a case study among Wang's reforms, seems to me particularly admirable. The service system was undoubtedly one of the most complicated institutions, if not indeed the most complicated institution, of the Sung period. And yet, within a chapter, the author has succeeded in presenting a very clear picture of the background, the significance of the new "hired service system," and the pros and cons for the new and old systems. This in itself is no mean achievement. With the other members of the Center for East Asian Studies, I take great pleasure in sponsoring this scholarly and stimulating volume.

Lien-sheng Yang

May 1959

Preface

Wang An-shih, the reformer of the eleventh century, is an outstanding figure in Chinese history. The New Policies, his response to the challenge of his time, bear such a striking resemblance to modern measures that they have been a source of inspiration in the contemporary world, not only to many Chinese in this period of vast change, but beyond China — for example, to the farm surplus policy of a country as far away as the United States of America. It is no exaggeration to suggest that Wang well deserves a place in world history.

Like many great figures in history, Wang has suffered from being imperfectly understood and even, not infrequently, perfectly misunderstood. Was Wang really an exceptional and radical reformer in the generally conservative development of Chinese history or did he, for all his remarkable qualities, remain well within the rich heritage of the Confucian tradition? Was he a great statesman with practical foresight, as those who admire him have claimed, or was he a misguided scholar, insistent upon his utopian ideas, as so many others who do not find him praiseworthy have maintained?

These and many other questions prompted me to attempt a reappraisal of this unusual man and his times. When a limited plan took definite shape a few years ago, the objective was to prepare a brief monograph. The outcome, as it now stands, is more than what was originally intended. Nonetheless, the task of reappraisal is still in an initial stage. New research on many problems concerning Wang and his period must yet be undertaken by many scholars before we can hope to understand this great historical figure in full measure.

Without the assistance of the program on Chinese Economic and Political Studies at Harvard University, this book could hardly have appeared so soon. My indebtedness to the individual members of this program goes beyond whatever feeble expression I may use. I am grateful to Professor Lien-sheng Yang for giving me initial encouragement and continuous guidance as well as for contributing his Foreword of the book. I also owe a great deal to Professor John K. Fairbank and Professor Benjamin I. Schwartz for their penetrating criticism and helpful suggestions. A sustaining friendship with Mr. Ch'ü T'ung-tsu, twice before my colleague and now at Harvard, has made my research pursuits so much more pleasant. Mrs. Elizabeth M. Matheson has performed an invaluable service in patiently going over the manuscript through more than one draft. Nor am I less thankful to the tireless librarian Dr. Alfred K. M. Ch'iu and the staff of the Harvard-Yenching Institute Library, where I have sought to reduce my ignorance through summer readings. In presenting these acknowledgments, my thoughts inevitably go back to Professor William Hung of Yenching University who initiated me into historical research in the days before World War II.

James Tzu-chien Liu

University of Pittsburgh
Pittsburgh, Pennsylvania

Contents

REFORM
IN SUNG CHINA

I

A Brief Account of Wang's Life
and the New Policies

In the long course of Chinese history few men stand out as prominently as Wang An-shih (1021–1086), the extraordinary reformer and most controversial statesman of the Northern Sung. The unconventional nature of the reform he introduced, the sweeping manner in which it was carried out, and the broad scope it encompassed were almost without precedent and were certainly without parallel until the last century. The specific reform measures, collectively known as the *hsin-fa*, have sometimes been referred to in translation as the New Laws. This translation, however, is unduly restrictive in meaning. The reform measures actually went far beyond the mere promulgation of new laws. They also included the establishing of new systems that brought about institutional changes. Perhaps they can be better described by the term New Policies, a more comprehensive designation which is closer to the facts.[1]

Since Wang has already been made well known through the studies of the Ch'ing scholar Ts'ai Shang-hsiang and of such modern scholars as Liang Ch'i-ch'ao, K'e Ch'ang-i, H. R. Williamson, and several others, there is no need here to give more than a brief account of his life and his reform measures.[2] Wang was a native of Lin-ch'uan, in the prefecture of Fuchou, in the modern province of Kiangsi, an area of rising national significance toward the middle of the Northern Sung period, with its increasing number of leading poets and essayists, esteemed scholars, and statesmen. Wang's family prospered in farming at the time of his great-grandfather. Turning to scholarship, it produced in the next three generations no less than eight holders of the doctorate degree (*chin-shih*), including Wang himself. Wang's father was a minor official who took his immediate family with him while serving in various local government posts. After his death in 1039 his family did not return to their native place but remained in Kiang-ning, modern Nanking.

Wang An-shih had a strong personality. As a young scholar with deep convictions he tended to choose only a few close friends with similar ideals, usually from the southern areas, specifically from Kiangsi and Fukien. This same tendency persisted throughout his life.

Wang's career began uneventfully. From 1042, when he earned his doctorate, until 1060, he chose to serve in local government posts not very far from Nanking — Yangchou in modern Kiangsu, Chenhsien in modern Chekiang, Suchou in modern Anhwei, and Ch'angchou, also in Kiangsu. He declined the opportunities to serve at the court that would have advanced his career but would not have enabled him to discharge his family and financial responsibilities. Nevertheless, his reputation spread as his scholarship became well known and his administrative ability was proven, especially in connection with irrigation works and financial measures. It was during his early career that he presented to Emperor Jen-tsung, in 1058, his "myriad word memorial" (*wan-yen-shu*). Though this memorial had no immediate consequences, it became the cornerstone of Wang's political theory, the basis of the reform which he later introduced, and a famous document in the history of Chinese political thought.

Wang's name gradually came to the attention of several high officials of varying political opinions. Through their repeated recommendations came offers of promotion; but he persistently refused them, always on the plea of family considerations. Not until 1060 was Wang finally prevailed upon to serve in the capital. After a brief term as a minor official in the Finance Commission (San-ssu), he was rapidly promoted, first to serve at the Imperial Chi-hsien Library and then to be a special drafting official of the Secretariat (Chih-chih-kao). These positions were among the ones regarded as "pure and respected offices" (ch'ing wang kuan), offices far removed from the "impure" duties involving financial or legal matters; but the holders of these positions were readily accessible to the emperor, not so much in connection with their administrative responsibilities as in the capacity of consultants, a capacity greatly respected by tradition. Such offices were generally reserved for highly recommended and promising scholar-officials.

Wang's advancement was soon interrupted by his observance of the mourning period for his mother from 1063 to 1066. Returning to government service in 1067, he became the governor of Nanking. It seemed as though he would long remain, of his own choice, in local government positions, but destiny dictated otherwise. A new emperor, Shen-tsung, succeeded to the throne in 1067. An alert and forward-looking man, he sought advice. Upon the recommendation of Han Wei (1017–1098), a former tutor of the Emperor, Wang was summoned to the court in early 1069. The Emperor was so impressed with him that he made him the second privy councilor (ts'an-chih-cheng-shih), a key position in which Wang was responsible for general administration. The Emperor accorded Wang unusual respect and trust and supported the reform which he instituted shortly thereafter.

Many important events and sweeping changes were crowded into the next few years when Wang was in power. Extensive irrigation works were undertaken on the Chang River, the Pien River and a section of the Yellow River, all mainly in the region around the Sung capital or in the modern province of Honan. Successful military campaigns were carried out in the northwest (the modern province of Kansu) around 1072; in the southwest (the modern province of Hunan) in 1073; and in the south (in repelling an invasion from Indochina) in 1076. All of these efforts and accomplishments were certainly noteworthy, but here we shall concentrate on the numerous reform measures that were instituted and that deeply affected government operations and institutions, as well as the livelihood of the people.[3] The following enumeration classifies the New Policies by areas in order to indicate the points of emphasis, and also the points at which complaints and opposition developed.[4] Many of these problem areas, of course, are interrelated and overlap.

Planning of state finance
1. Establishment of the Finance Planning Commission, in the second month of 1069, to study and recommend the reorganization of state finance.

State financing for farmers
2. The Farming Loans, the so-called Young-Shoots Money, instituted in the ninth month of 1069, to be extended to the farmers upon sowing and to be repaid with interest at harvest time.

State revenues and maintenance
3. Tribute revenues. The Tribute Transport and Distribu-

tion System, introduced in the seventh month of 1069, governing the transportation, exchange, selling, and buying of the tributary items normally sent to the government from the provinces, in order to anticipate government needs and stabilize prices.

4. Local government maintenance. The Hired-Service System, made effective for the whole nation, after experimentation in the capital, in the tenth month of 1070, assessing a graduated cash tax to pay for the hiring of necessary personnel to render services for the local government, which had previously been carried on by rotating assignment of corvée duties.

5. Maintenance of local order. The *Pao-chia* System, introduced in the twelfth month of 1070, organizing rural inhabitants in basic units of ten families or more, to assume collective responsibility for community policing duties.

6. Land tax. The Land Survey and Equitable Tax, effective in the eighth month of 1072, aiming at the elimination of tax evasion and unfair burdens, especially in the northern areas.

National defense

7. The basic measure. The *Pao-chia* System and its eventual use to raise army reserve units, by a system akin to conscription.

8. Other improvements. The Horse-Breeding System, beginning in the fifth month of 1072, assigning a horse with fodder to each family in frontier regions in the north and the northwest; establishment of the Directorate of Weapons, in the sixth month of 1073, to improve the quality of weapons; and other minor measures to strengthen military defense.

Currency

9. Removal of the ban on private shipment and handling of copper, in the seventh month of 1070, and increased government mintage of copper coins on several occasions to meet the demand created by the expanded state financing and the requirements of cash tax payments.

Trade

10. State Trade System, introduced in the third month of 1072, by which the government purchased commodities directly from the smaller merchants and extended loan facilities to them so that they did not have to deal through the guilds. Through this system the government intended to stabilize market prices.

11. Guild Exemption Tax, effective in the ninth month of 1073, a cash assessment of the various guilds, which were thus exempted from the customary burden of contributing supplies to the palace.

Education and civil service

12. Education. Reorganization of the National Academy (sometimes translated as the National University), in the ninth month of 1071, so that it would eventually replace the examination system; establishment of new classes there and schools elsewhere in the capital for training in such specialized fields as military science, law, and medicine; and also the establishment of many prefectural schools, especially in the northern areas where promotion of education had been lacking.

13. Examination system. Placement of emphasis on problems, policy discussions, and interpretations of the classics, rather than on poetry and rhymed prose, in the regular doctoral examinations, beginning in the

third month of 1070; and the instituting of law as a new field among those of the lesser degrees.

14. Appointment to offices. Introduction, in the third month of 1073, of a test in law for the holders of the doctorate degree, sponsored candidates, and other persons eligible for appointment.

15. Government clerks. Clerks who had no official rank put on a salary basis, in the twelfth month of 1070, and placed under strict supervision with due punishment for misconduct; also, meritorious clerks promoted to minor officials, after passing a test.

In taking charge of state affairs as the leading court minister and in introducing his New Policies, Wang's greatest difficulty was lack of cooperation among the majority of the bureaucrats. Opposition to his policies came from many prominent officials: to mention but a few, Han Ch'i (1008–1075) and Fu Pi (1004–1083), the venerated elder statesmen who had earlier been responsible for the first, but minor, reform of 1043–1044; Ou-yang Hsiu (1007–1072), another elder statesman who had previously recommended Wang; Lü Kung-chu (1018–1089), a leader among the politically prominent families who had praised and befriended Wang; Ssu-ma Kuang (1019–1086), a greatly respected scholar-official who commanded the support of many conservatives in the northern areas; the Su brothers, Su Shih (1036–1101) and Su Ch'e (1039–1112), the brilliant leaders from the southwestern area of Szechwan; and even Cheng Hsia (1041–1119), who had studied under Wang and supported him at the beginning of the reform. But the widespread opposition deterred neither Wang nor the Emperor. Wang, promoted to first privy councilor (*t'ung chung-shu men-hsia p'ing-chang shih*) in 1071, continued to exercise a dominant influence at the court and persuaded the Emperor to demote his outspoken opponents one after another.

A decisive turn in Wang's career came with his temporary resignation from the court in 1074. The famine in the northern areas aggravated whatever sufferings the people had endured under the reform system. The opposition renewed their attacks with increased vigor, and the Emperor was deeply shocked when Cheng Hsia presented a memorial that gave a dramatic "portrait of the refugees" (*liu-min-t'u*) from the famine areas. At the same time, the State Trade System and the Guild Exemption Tax created discontent in the capital city of K'ai-feng which led the palace people, principally the Empress Dowager Hsüan-jen, and the eunuchs, to warn the Emperor against Wang. Wang's feelings and pride were greatly injured, and he resigned. The Emperor, who still had considerable confidence in him, made him the governor of Nanking, with the honorary rank of titular councilor. On the other hand, the Emperor for the first time expressed some uncertainty about the reform by ordering the temporary suspension of certain controversial measures and asking for frank criticism of them.

Wang was not long absent from the capital; he was restored to his leading place at the court in less than a year, in early 1075. However, his second term in power found him in a much weaker political position than before. Many of his recommendations no longer met with the ready approval of the Emperor. His two principal associates were demoted and left the court, having incurred his displeasure: Tseng Pu (1035–1107) for having exposed, against Wang's wishes, the faults of the state trade system and the guild exemption tax, and thus indirectly contributing to Wang's earlier resignation; and Lü Hui-ch'ing (1031–1111) for having sought to undermine Wang's influence during his absence from the court.

The men to whom he now turned for support were much less experimental and, worse, far less trustworthy. The reform continued, but so did the persistent opposition to it. Wang himself became depressed, particularly after the death of his only and much beloved son, Wang Fang. The Emperor finally allowed Wang to retire in the winter of 1076.

In retirement Wang devoted himself principally to the writing of a book on etymology, *Tzu shuo*. The Emperor honored him highly by making him the Duke of Shu-kuo, and he had the sustaining satisfaction of seeing his reform system continue without major change for another nine years, until the death of Emperor Shen-tsung in 1085 brought the reform to an end. Wang died the following year, greatly saddened by the sudden turn of the political tide which demolished his reform system.

To complete this brief narrative, one must go beyond the reform phase of 1069–1085 to the antireform of 1085–1093 and the postreform of 1093–1125.[5] The antireform phase occurred under the regency of Empress Dowager Hsüan-jen. One after another, many of the New Policies were rescinded or drastically revised. Prominent reform supporters were formally denounced as the members of an undesirable faction (*tang*). Even some of the conservatives, like Fan Ch'un-jen, Su Shih, and Su Ch'e, who objected to the swing to the other extreme, were out of favor. The death of Ssu-ma Kuang, who led the conservatives at the beginning of this phase, left the power in the hands of Lü Kung-chu, Lü Ta-fang (1028–1097), and Liu Chih (1030–1097). Their common dislike of the New Policies did not prevent them from disagreeing on other matters and dividing into personal cliques.

The postreform phase began in 1093, when the Empress Dowager died and Emperor Che-tsung himself took up the reins of government. He recalled to power those who had supported the New Policies, led by Chang Ch'un (1034–1105), Wang An-shih's son-in-law Ts'ai Pien, and his brother Ts'ai Ching (1046–1126). Most of the New Policies were revived and several were extended in application to additional geographic regions. A revengeful political persecution on a large scale sent hundreds of the conservatives to humiliating local government posts far away. One notable exception to the prevailing political climate occurred in 1100 when Emperor Chetsung was succeeded by his brother Hui-tsung. Tseng Pu, the only one of Wang's early associates to regain some measure of leadership, introduced a policy of reconciliation and unity by naming the reign "Establishment of a Middle Course" (Chienchung) and by recommending some conservatives to high offices, in the hope of ameliorating factional antagonism. Unfortunately, this short-lived policy failed to please the other leaders of the postreform or to appease the embittered conservatives. The one who successfully contrived to secure domination over all the rest was Ts'ai Ching. He remained in power, with only brief interruptions, for nearly a quarter of a century, from 1101 to 1125, just two years before the invasion of the Chin army ended the Northern Sung dynasty. Under him the political persecution intensified, corruption increased, and the government administration deteriorated in many ways. The reform went down in history in bad repute as a result of the earlier complaints against it, the unceasing denunciation of the conservatives, and, significantly, the criticism that it led directly to the notorious postreform that was identified with the fall of the dynasty.

II

Problems of Interpretation

The bitterness of the controversies over the reform and the turns of the political tide that followed it make the historical study of this complicated era exceedingly difficult. Many of the primary sources suffer from both biased statements and deliberate omissions. To begin with, the draft and the redraft of the *Shih-lu* (Veritable Records, sometimes known as the Reign Chronicles) generated heated debates during the antireform and the postreform phases. The third and last draft, prepared in the early Southern Sung period but no longer extant,[1] finally settled the issue in favor of the antireform view. This version was prepared by men who deeply resented the postreform mal-administration.[2] It also accorded with the explicit wishes of Empress Dowager Chao-tz'u, the consort of Che-tsung. Chao-tz'u supported the Empress Dowager Hsüan-jen, who had abrogated the reform, and she was so disliked by her husband, the succeeding emperor, that she was banished from the palace in connection with the postreform revenge and palace intrigues.[3] Spared captivity by the Chin conquerors, who attempted un-successfully to solicit the support of the conservative elements,[4] she eventually rejoined the court of the Southern Sung in great honor and came to be regarded as the surviving symbol of the Northern Sung regime as well as of the better days be-fore the postreform. It was Chao-tz'u who asked the Emperor

Kao-tsung to tell the compilers of the *Shih-lu* to place responsibility for the disastrous fall of the Northern Sung on Ts'ai Ching and his associates.[5] However, in the final draft of the *Shih-lu,* this purposeful condemnation of the postreform was intermingled with the scholars' long-standing prejudice against Wang and his reform. It was an injustice to Wang that stemmed in part from a mistaken association of Wang with the postreform.

Fortunately for history, Li T'ao in 1174 privately compiled the *Hsü tzu-chih-t'ung-chien ch'ang-pien* (HCP), a voluminous collection of source materials, both official and otherwise with minimal editorial revisions, chronologically arranged for the eventual preparation of an annalistic history of the Northern Sung. This compilation, although it shows some antireform bias, may safely be used in conjunction with the *Sung hui-yao chi-kao* (SHY) the repository of selected government documents; these two works are the best primary sources.[6]

The *Sung-shih* (SS), or the Sung dynastic history, compiled during the Yüan period, is of generally inferior quality and is particularly unfair to the reform.[7] Its chief compilers relied heavily upon the writings of Chu Hsi, the influential Southern Sung philosopher, whose opinions on Wang and the reform, though sometimes kind, were basically unfavorable.[8] When drafts presented different views, the chief compilers of the Sung dynastic history never hesitated to make changes that conformed to their own views.[9] Other standard compilations on Sung history generally show improvements over the Sung dynastic history, but they fail to rectify the bias against the reform.

The miscellaneous writings (*pi-chi*) by private individuals that appeared shortly after Wang's death and during the Southern Sung must be handled with great care. Not a few of them contain gossip, slander, and even fabrications.[10] The

intense rivalry for fame among some of the scholar-officials
of the period contributed to the growth of an exposé literature, which is incidentally an interesting body of literature
worthy of future research. Much more useful than the miscellaneous writings are the collected works (*wen-chi*) of
many leading scholar-officials. The information they provide,
being much more reliable, has been used by recent researchers
to supplement the data given in the HCP and SHY; and the
use of these collections is far from exhausted.

Research on Wang began belatedly with the detailed biographical study by the Ch'ing scholar Ts'ai Shang-hsiang, who
spared no effort to demolish the historical prejudice against
Wang and the reform that had persisted since the Southern
Sung. It was this significant work that enabled modern scholars like Liang Ch'i-ch'ao to reintroduce Wang to the present
century as a great hero by emphasizing his farsightedness and
the resemblance of his New Policies to modern ideals. In the
1930's K'e Ch'ang-i and H. R. Williamson in their well-
known works on Wang, one in Chinese and the other in
English, amplified essentially the same thesis with additional
materials. The work by K'e has made some, though not extensive, use of the HCP. These two studies have been regarded for some time as probably the standard works. However, the publication in 1936 of the SHY, which at once substantiates the reliability of the HCP and reveals a great deal
of further information, immediately outdated all the previous
works on Wang.

Recent scholars have not yet attempted a comprehensive
study of Wang and the reform. They have been more inclined
to devote themselves to detailed studies of specific reform
measures, one by one. They are keenly aware that Wang and
the reform can only be understood in the broad frame of
reference of his period and the various developmental trends

of Sung society. In this regard, important contributions have been made by many scholars, notably the following: Ch'üan Han-sheng on economic history, Miyazaki Ichisada on government and political behavior, Nieh Ch'ung-ch'i on government institutions and political history, Sogabe Shizuo on finance, and Sudō Yoshiyuki on the land system and bureaucratic social mobility.

The attention of the recent scholars in the field of Sung history, collectively speaking, has been given first to the economic development and second to the political institutions. Relatively little has been done on Sung thought. Studies in this last field generally stress the metaphysical and the self-cultivationist philosophies that began to develop in the Northern Sung and became predominant in the Southern Sung. Conversely, there has been a neglect of the political theories, especially those with a utilitarian emphasis, that were influential during the Northern Sung. Hsiao Kung-ch'üan, while not a Sung specialist, deserves credit for assigning due weight to this aspect in his general history of Chinese political thought.[11]

From all this literature emerge diverse interpretations of Wang and his reform. In the traditional historiography Wang has been regarded as a brilliant scholar, an honest but obstinate statesman, misguided by his excessive self-confidence and his misplaced trust in unworthy associates. In this view, Wang cannot be considered a foremost Confucianist in the orthodox sense. On the other hand, the detailed study by Ts'ai Shang-hsiang contends that this is a misunderstanding, if not a distortion, and that Wang should be regarded as a true and indeed an extraordinary Confucianist.

The publications of the present century, needless to say, no longer base their interpretations of Wang on Confucian grounds. Liang, in his biographical work, emphasizes Wang's ideals and reform measures that aim at "enriching the nation (or the state) and strengthening the army" (*fu-kuo ch'iang-ping*).[12] Other authors, for example, J. C. Ferguson, appraise Wang in the light of modern liberalism. Yet others, notably Williamson, compare Wang's reform to state socialism.[13] In the current era, charged with a nationalistic and revolutionary spirit, the popular interpretations of Wang tend to overglorify him. Only one rare exception, expressing a minority view, regards Wang as "dictatorial," and this work, not being very judicious in its use of historical sources, need not be taken too seriously.[14] In any event, these varied interpretations have one common characteristic: they examine Wang retrospectively through modern glasses and from the particular political viewpoint held by the author.

Research scholars in more recent years have invariably drawn attention to the general developments during the Sung period, with particular emphasis on the socio-economic trends, these socio-economic trends they have used as a basis for interpreting political trends, such as the ones reflected in Wang's reform measures. These scholars stress the vested interests of the scholar-official class in its landownership and privileges. They suggest that in such vested interests lies the clue that explains the bureaucratic character and the absolutist nature of the Sung empire. While they do not deny that Wang was a reformer, praiseworthy, idealistic, and extraordinary, they feel that it would be a mistake and an undue glorification to regard him as an exceptional statesman rising above the socio-economic context of his time.

Two hypotheses are emphasized in the more recent interpretations of Wang and his era that have been offered by such scholars as Naitō Torajirō, Wang Yü-ch'üan, Sudō Yoshiyuki, and several other Japanese researchers who follow Sudō's line of inquiry. The first is that Wang represents the interests of the newly risen medium-sized landowners (located mainly in the southern areas) in a surging and vigorous struggle against the vested interests of large-scale landlords (mainly in the northern areas) and the large and monopolistic merchants. The second is that the New Policies in effect expanded the power of the bureaucratic class as a whole and tightened the control of the absolutist state.[15]

These two hypotheses are not necessarily in disagreement. It has been suggested that a close relationship may be seen to exist between the interests of the medium-sized landowners and the interests of the absolutist state. On the one hand, the medium-sized landowners value the protection of the state; on the other hand, the medium-sized landholding probably accords best with the interests of the absolutist state itself.[16] However, this coincidence of interest by no means implies a complete identity of interest. The recent research of many scholars has effectively demonstrated that the bureaucrats played a double role in serving simultaneously the interests of both the medium-sized landholders and of the absolutist state. No study has yet been made of the choices made by some bureaucrats when these two sets of interests conflicted. Wang through his New Policies probably tried to serve the best interests of the state as he idealized them, sometimes even at the expense of the class to which he belonged by social origin.[17] Yet many of his followers probably identified themselves less with the state's interests than with their class, if not their personal, interests.

The recent interpretations so far have clarified considerably, though not yet conclusively, the general socio-economic trends of the time. It is still questionable whether the class-interest hypotheses in these interpretations are fully supported by factual findings; alternatively it is possible that the socio-economic trends posited by such hypotheses, if substantiated, will offer sufficient explanations of the political trends. While socio-economic factors unquestionably influence political trends, there are other factors which also play their part and these have to be assessed. The recent interpretations have not given enough attention, for instance, to the diverse lines of thought or political philosophies which divided the scholar-officials into different and opposing schools. Furthermore, political trends have dynamics of their own. To the same socio-economic setting and even within one given school of thought, scholar-officials respond with different political behavior. Such behavior provides a basis for classifying them into distinctive bureaucratic types.[18] In short, the recent interpretations, though enlightening and helpful, still leave considerable room for a reappraisal.

THE PRESENT REAPPRAISAL AND ITS FRAME OF REFERENCE

The present inquiry involves a reappraisal of Wang and his time within a political context. First, it will review the research published in the last quarter of a century by many Japanese, some Chinese, and a few American scholars, either on Wang and his New Policies or on the significant developments of this period. There are a few outstanding books and a great many articles that should be brought to the attention of all interested students. Secondly, it will seek to bring together, the various interpretations, insofar as they are compatible, in order to gain a comprehensive understanding of Wang and his time. This reappraisal will draw upon the various interpretations in terms of political thought, political behavior, and government operations, including researches of my own. It is hoped that the use of this political frame of reference, which is different from the socio-economic context generally used by many contemporary scholars, may help to establish new points of departure for further investigation.

Such a political approach necessitates a rapid survey of the political setting, with its relevant social and economic background. The Northern Sung period, as Kracke has aptly described it, experienced many epoch-making "changes within the tradition" of China.[19]

With the advancement of education and the wide use of printing, learning reached new heights and a creative diversity appeared within the Confucian uniformity. The southern areas, from the Yangtze River valley down to the coast of Fukien, were significantly bidding for a leading position in the nation, not only in terms of population, productivity, trade, and general prosperity, but also in terms of education and scholarship. Urban modes of living spread from the metropolitan areas and sizable cities. Mony economy slowly but steadily expanded. Political trends paralleled these social and economic developments. Sogabe Shizuo has pointed out that the Sung empire compensated for its military weakness by its economic strength. Ironically, however, it sagged under the heavy weight of the financial burden imposed by defense exigencies and a large bureaucracy.[20]

The key role in these epoch-making changes belonged to the scholar-official or bureaucratic class. As scholars, they produced an intellectual diversification through the formation of new theories, through new interpretations of the Confucian classics, and through their varying emphases upon different strands in the Confucian heritage.[21] Several different schools of thought vied with one another in claiming a new orthodoxy in Confucianism.

As officials they held a much stronger political position than had the officials under previous dynasties. Many of them were quite content with their careers, prestige, and privileges;

others relaxed their Confucian discipline and deviated from behavioral norms in one way or another. Below the officials were the clerks (*li* or *hsü-li*), who were not a part of the bureaucracy but formed a subbureaucracy of their own, especially those who served in the local government offices of their native areas. Having little hope of promotion into officialdom and being confined mainly to their existing positions, these clerks were always looking for loopholes in the administration whereby they might profit at the expense of both the government and the common people. The inertia in the entire administration would have remained undisturbed but for the activities of two kinds of officials, the idealistic and the manipulative. The zealous officials who were idealistic and interested in general improvement sought the reform of the bureaucracy, and sometimes that of the subbureaucracy, as a necessary step to carry out their policies. The manipulative officials, who were ambitious but not interested in general improvement, wanted to gain power and control in the bureaucracy, mainly in terms of their career and personal interests. Both groups, the good and the bad, initiated power struggles and provoked intense opposition.

The major cause of the power struggle at the court was the centralizing tendency of the Northern Sung government. Other contributary causes were the rise (or upward social mobility) of new bureaucrats from the south, who were replacing bureaucrats of large-sized landowning background in the north; the ever-increasing number of officials, protective appointees (*yin-pu*) who were the family members and relatives of high-ranking officials, degree-holders, and other candidates — all competing for better positions; and finally, the different schools of thought and the diverse opinions on policy matters, which helped to put a premium on criticism and impeachment and filled the political atmosphere with endless charges and countercharges. The intensity of this power struggle was evidenced by nepotism, by the formation of personal cliques often but not always based upon differences in political outlook, and by the clash of the bitterly divided factions on policy matters. Another evidence was an abundance of political communication, larger in volume perhaps than ever before: copies of argumentative and supercritical memorials, partisan and denunciatory official documents, private correspondence engaging in heated debate, informal writings indulging in slander and even in fabrications and forgery. Many of these were circulated informally through social contacts, deliberately as political ammunition, and commercially in circles eager for news and gossip, especially at the capital and in other large cities.[22]

The advancement of the scholar-official class to an unprecedented prestige was one of the splendors of the Sung empire. Yet, this neither negated absolutism nor precluded it from slowly gaining strength, particularly toward the end of the Northern Sung. In fact, a tension always existed between the rising power of the ranking officials, to whom the emperor must of necessity delegate some power, and the carefully guarded ultimate power of the emperor himself. The more bitter the power struggle among the bureaucrats became, the greater was the probability of their depending upon the support of the emperor, of their playing into the hands of those around the emperor and in the palace, and of their helping, by design or by force of circumstances, the growth of absolutism. The growth of absolutism in turn enforced a greater degree of bureaucratic conformity. In the long run absolutism and conformity made the bureaucratic class more subservient.

Economically, the bureaucrats by law had certain privileges of exemption from tax and service. Some of them exceeded these privileges by indulging in tax evasions and corrupt practices, with the connivance of local officials and clerks. Any state policies aimed at improvement of the overstrained government finance would inevitably affect in one way or another the private interests of all the bureaucrats, privileged or abusive, whether they were large or small landowners.

The growth of money economy and trade activities created further division among the bureaucrats. An alert minority, more accustomed to these developments, sought to introduce new features into state financing, such as tax payment in cash, government operations in trading, and restrictions upon the activities of the large merchants. The majority, bound by bureaucratic inertia and orthodox Confucian ideas, opposed these new features and argued for the traditional policy of no government interference with trade activities. Some bureaucrats took the consumers' viewpoint against monopolistic merchants, while others were friendly toward the merchants, perhaps because they had either indirect connections with the merchants through their family backgrounds or a direct interest through their own private trade activities.

It was upon this complex political scene, with its social and economic concomitants, that Wang appeared. His thought and his actions were responses to the political environment as he found it. His New Policies were conceived to improve it; yet their implementation was inevitably conditioned by it, and the controversy over them added further complications. An analysis of Wang and his New Policies in terms of political thought, political behavior, and government operations can therefore help considerably to clarify the involved political situation of Wang's day, although of course numerous aspects of the total picture have yet to be adequately explored.

III

Wang and the Political Thought
of the Northern Sung

DIVERSITY IN EARLY NEO-CONFUCIANISM

Wang was an outstanding thinker as well as an unusual statesman. He appeared at a time of ferment, marked by fresh
thinking on the part of many rising Confucianists, and his
thought must be examined against the background of that of
his predecessors and contemporaries.

The Sung Confucianists believed that they had reached a
new height in the best tradition of Confucianism, surpassing
the attainments of both the Han and the T'ang periods. This
belief was not without factual basis, for they did strive toward
new horizons, explore new depths, introduce new contents,
and hold forth new formulations, though all of these were
new only in the relative sense within the broad frame of the
Confucian heritage — hence the term Neo-Confucianism. The
early days of Neo-Confucianism during the Northern Sung
period presented a remarkable diversity which expressed itself in several distinct trends. While all the Confucianists at
the time agreed upon a common base, they developed varying
formulations. While interested in the same range of subjects,
they frequently differed with regard to emphasis and interpretation. While all were dedicated to the proposition that a
moral society is the ultimate goal of government, they advocated different approaches toward the realization of this

ideal. Among the diverse elements a dispute gradually arose as to which should be accepted as the orthodoxy.

Wang's thought occupied a significant place in this diversity but it eventually suffered an almost complete defeat in the hard and bitter struggle for orthodoxy. Influential as it was for a time, especially when Wang himself was in power, it soon became discredited through the failure of reform attempts to attain their objectives, through increasing partisan attacks and political disfavor, and finally through the poor conduct of those later followers who claimed a nominal allegiance to it without carrying out its principles in earnest. By the time of the Southern Sung it was practically dismissed as an unwarranted offshoot that deviated from Confucianism, while the thought and teachings of many others who were opposed to Wang were respected and honored as the foundations of the Neo-Confucian orthodoxy.

To do justice to Wang's thought, we must return to the diversity of the Northern Sung period, of which it was a part, and which may be briefly described in two ways: first, in terms of distinctive trends of thought, and then in terms of an evolutionary process — the development of political theories, the rise of separate schools, and their conflicts not only in thought but in political action.

There were three distinctive trends. The first, to use the term introduced by Hsiao, led toward utilitarian political theories. This was probably the most energetic and assertive of the trends even before the appearance of Wang, who brought it to its culmination.[1] Its foremost concern was with the pressing tasks of statecraft: fiscal policies, economic measures, national defense, an effective administrative system, and other practical matters. It was a direct response to the strained finances of the government, the expansion of trade in the country, the military weakness of the state, and the apparent incapacity of the bureaucracy to cope successfully with the situation.

The second trend placed a fundamental emphasis upon personal morality and a profound belief in the value of self-realization. While by no means excluding utilitarian considerations, it emphasized that moral principles must be held paramount and observed strictly. It did not deny the existence of urgent problems, but insisted upon the need for sound solutions and the avoidance of hasty and ill-conceived measures. The most essential qualifications of statecraft are the moral leadership and influence of upright officials. Only these qualifications can in the long run lead to the careful formulation of proper policies and their faithful execution.

The third trend had the same emphasis but went one step further. Its distinction lay in developing a metaphysical basis of morality which greatly strengthened the belief that moral values were of more fundamental importance than utilitarian values. These last two trends, affiliated with one another, finally converged during the Southern Sung period to establish the orthodoxy of Neo-Confucianism.

Early Neo-Confucianism, of which diversity, rather than orthodoxy, was the keynote, may be more concretely described in terms of the evolution of political theories into separate schools, which in effect became political factions involved in a great dispute of thought as well as government policies. This evolutionary process underwent three stages: the initial stage, the stage of development, and the stage of conflict. These three stages succeeded one another rapidly within a decade or two, often overlapping.

The initial stage began under the stable reign of Chen-tsung (997–1022) when early Neo-Confucianism came forward with political ideals and demanded national attention. The leading exponents, Hu Yüan (993–1059) and Sun Fu

(992–1057), were typically professional teachers rather than high officials. Their political ideals found some limited expression in the first reform of the Sung period in 1043–1044, led by Fan Chung-yen (989–1052). Hu Yüan, who started his teaching in Hu-chou in the Yangtze delta region, stressed the relation between the interpretations of the classics and their direct application to current problems of statecraft. His contribution lay largely in the promotion of this general outlook, which encouraged many scholars throughout the country to discuss political theories.[2] He himself did not found any particular school. Sun Fu, on the other hand, established a separate school of thought in Shantung province and its influence was extended by followers who taught in the areas on both sides of the Yellow River. His school emphasized metaphysics based on the Book of Changes (I-ching), as well as proper status, correct relationship, and moral self-realization based on another classic, the Spring and Autumn Annals (Ch'un-ch'iu).[3] It was these emphases that led the northern scholars who came after Sun Fu to further development in the areas of metaphysics or moral philosophy, often in both, in the conviction that these were more important than the search for utilitarian policies.

The stage of advancement had two outstanding characteristics. The first was the rising standard and the increasing comprehensiveness of scholarship. This was best illustrated by the astounding example of Ou-yang Hsiu (1007–1072) who found time in his active political career to distinguish himself as a highly respected authority in many fields of scholarly pursuit: the classics, history, political theory, poetry, prose, and even a number of specialized fields such as archaeology. Many of his ideas became points of departure from which those who came under his influence formulated various political opinions, thus contributing to the diversity of the

period. His personality made his influence ever greater, for
he was actively interested in promoting many promising young
scholars, who in turn strove toward still higher standards in
several directions.[4] The second characteristic of this stage was
the appearance of unconventional theories. The leading ex-
ponent of unconventional theories was Li Kou (1009–1059)
who came from the same area of Kiangsi as both Ou-yang
Hsiu and Wang An-shih. Though Li Kou expounded moral
virtues, which had due influence upon the scholars in the
north, he attracted far greater attention from some of the
scholars in the south by his fervently utilitarian views. For
example, Li Kou regarded the Chou Rites (*Chou-li*) as the
classic that outlines the best principles of government. He
maintained that some of these principles should be applied
for the purpose of "enriching the state and strengthening the
army," an objective that the conventional Confucianists generally opposed as a Legalist one. Such utilitarian views,
radical as they were, had a powerful influence upon Wang,
who held the Chou Rites in even greater reverence than did
Li. We shall return to this significant point in the next section. However, it is pertinent to mention here that Wang did
not follow Li Kou entirely. For instance, Li Kou rejected
Mencius for having many mistaken notions on the ways to
reintroduce or revitalize ancient systems. But Wang paid high
tribute to Mencius for his utilitarian position in believing that
the economic welfare of the people is of great importance and
that morality cannot be separated from prosperity, both being
the indispensable conditions of a good social order.[5] It is clear
that in the general diversity of thought, this particular trend
was gaining momentum from Hu Yüan, through Li Kou, to
Wang. Hu Yüan favored the application of the classics to
practical matters in general. Li Kou advocated the application
of one classic in particular, with a strong utilitarian interpreta-

tion. Wang went on to include some other classics, with an
even greater emphasis on utilitarian values.

The third and last stage in the evolution was that of conflict.
It occurred when Wang was in power. There now appeared
four schools of thought which disagreed vigorously with one
another and whose disagreements were further complicated
and aggravated by regional rivalries, differences in socio-economic background, and political exigencies.

Wang was the leader of the New School (Hsin Hsüeh),
a name derived from his New Policies. Most followers of
this school came from Kiangsi and Fukien. As the research of
Sudō and of several other scholars indicates, they usually
came from successful farming families whose bureaucratic
background was of relatively recent origin.[6] In this school the
utilitarian trend reached its climax.

The second group was the Shuo School, Shuo meaning the
areas north of the Yellow River. It had the most conservative
intellectual and political outlook. It believed that moral leadership is the basic principle of government, and that when
moral leadership was added to the existing policies or the
political and economic systems in general, conditions would
be greatly improved. They were unalterably opposed to the
New Policies which to them meant both a disregard of moral
leadership and an unwarranted disturbance of the old and
stable order.

The third group was the Lo School, the name taken from
its stronghold, the city of Loyang, well known for its aristocratic heritage. The school had another center to the west in
Shensi province. In other words, its geographic base lay immediately below the Yellow River. Some of its leaders received
their early education in the south, a number of its followers
came directly from the south, and the school on the whole
shared some common roots and ideas with the New School,

but it did not at all agree with the approach or the emphases of the New School. The Lo School encouraged the study of metaphysics in addition to self-realization, which in its very essence embodies the metaphysical principles and translates them into moral qualities. It believed that such self-realization would naturally manifest itself in achieving good social order and government. While this school turned out to be the fore-runner of the Neo-Confucian orthodoxy of the Southern Sung period, it did not in its own day hold supremacy over the other schools. Owing to its emphasis on metaphysics, many of its members did not actively engage in politics; those who did generally sided with the members of the Shuo School, though they were not nearly so conservative as the latter.[7] The Lo School opposed the New Policies primarily because it believed that the New Policies had gone astray and had put many unscrupulous persons into power.

Roughly speaking, therefore, the Lo School and the Shuo School may be grouped together as the northern conserva-tives, with the understanding that the latter was the more typical respresentative of the North both in the geographic sense and in the political and intellectual connotation of the word "northern" at the time.

The fourth and last group was the Shu School, Shu being the name of the Szechwan area in the southwest. Its moral philosophy had a touch of Buddhist influence and of Taoist romanticism. Its political theories were noted more for their argumentative brilliance than for their systematic profundity. Both of these traits were traceable to Ou-yang Hsiu. Though the members of this school also stood with the conservatives in common opposition to the New Policies, they were more often than not the moderates. They agreed in part on the need to emphasize the utilitarian aspects of government poli-cies. But they did not agree that changes should be drastic or radical, or that they should be undertaken without careful weighing and without men of good character to administer them. On the other hand, many members of this school criticized the northern schools for having dogmatically gone to the other extreme.[8] This criticism was not inspired solely by a difference in political opinion; it also stemmed from a basic difference in the concept of self-realization. Self-realization, in the moral philosophy of leaders of this school like Su Shih, should include a natural humaneness, somewhat akin to the Taoist spirit, as a counterweight to self-righteousness, doctrinaire inflexibility, and excessive severity, which often set the leaders apart from the common people. But in opposing the New Policies and in criticizing the northern conservatives at the same time, the moderates tended to be supercritics who had few constructive alternatives to offer. Since this school was in the minority, politically and intellectually, the stage centered mainly around the struggle between the New School and the northern conservatives.

Before we proceed further to discuss in detail the differences between the reformers and the conservatives, it is appropriate to offer a concluding remark on the diversity of early Neo-Confucianism. However much the leaders of these four schools differed in their interpretations of the Confucian classics, they were all serious scholars. No matter how their political theories clashed, most of them were so devoted to their respective beliefs that political principles generally took precedence over considerations of self-interest. Among many of them differences of opinion did not preclude mutual respect, though in many cases it did lead to mutual dislike and even to personal attacks questioning whether a political enemy's moral standing was really worthy of a Confucian scholar.

The leaders were by no means faultless. While the Chinese historians traditionally honored them by the designation "virtuous men" (*chün-tzu*), their actual behavior, as Miyazaki Ichisada has pointed out, in many respects, certainly fell short of the idealized standards that this designation theoretically implies. To be fair, however, at least the majority of them were morally upright, maintained a high degree of personal integrity, and observed rather closely the Confucian virtues.[9] Above all, they demonstrated in accordance with their respective beliefs a commendable amount of political idealism. These were the worthy qualities common to the leading scholar-officials of various schools, despite the diversity among them, in a great period of Confucianism. It was these qualities that distinguished them as idealistic scholar-officials, and as far superior to the ordinary career-minded bureaucrats who, whatever political ideals they happened to profess, usually subordinated them to their selfish interests and personal gains.[10]

THE DIFFERENCES BETWEEN THE REFORMERS
AND THE CONSERVATIVES

The major source of conflict between the southern reformers led by Wang and the northern conservatives who vigorously opposed his New Policies was their divergent political theories. However, related to this ideological divergence there were a number of other factors which tended to divide them. Some attention should therefore be given to the differences in their respective religious, socio-political, and economic backgrounds.

The differing political theories of the two groups created at least three theoretical issues in connection with the interpretation of the Confucian classics. The first and probably the most significant issue concerned the *Chou-li* versus the *Ch'un-*

ch'iu. The question was, of these two classics, which was the more valuable as the basis of political principle. The *Chou-li* has had a remarkable connection with several reform attempts and movements at different times in Chinese history. The earliest case was its influence on Wang Mang, the usurper-emperor in the middle of the Han period. The most recent cases were the T'aip'ing rebellion in the middle of the nineteenth century. The book also had a significant influence on Wang's political thought and the formulation of his New Policies. The *Chou-li* exerted a strong influence in all these cases principally because of its utopian nature. It extols the ancient Chou period by showing the active leadership of the state in setting up a number of political, economic, and social systems which regulated these respective phases of the people's life. It was this highly idealized picture of a perfect order that furnished inspiration and theoretical justification to those who endeavored to discard the existing systems in favor of new ones. Shortly before Wang became a prominent scholar-official, Li Kou had already called attention to the importance of this book. Li Kou, as we have mentioned, favored the application of the principles outlined in the *Chou-li* for the sake of "enriching the state and strengthening the army," which he believed to be an urgent necessity for the Sung empire. Wang agreed with Li Kou that the book not only describes many ideal systems but presents the best view of the roles of government. But Wang's emphasis was different from Li's. Wang considered political order, fiscal policies, and economic welfare to be more important than military strength. Yet his general reliance upon the *Chou-li* met with objections from the conservatives. To the conservatives, the ancient systems described in the book neither could be sufficiently understood nor properly applied to existing conditions.[11] The conservatives were particularly offended when

Wang made his own interpretation of the *Chou-li* the standard version for the state examination, thereby imposing it upon many aspiring scholar-officials.

The conservatives were equally offended when Wang eliminated from the state examination the classic *Ch'un-ch'iu* which had long been a specialized field of study. To the conservatives, who followed both Sun Fu and Ou-yang Hsiu in this respect, the *Ch'un-ch'iu* was the principal classic for the guidance of political behavior. It set the example of judging conduct by the moral principles affirmed by Confucius himself, moral principles which were held to be eternally applicable and universally true.[12] But Wang and his followers offered objections. The *Ch'un-ch'iu*, according to a famous quotation attributed to Wang, possibly by his enemies, seemed like "worthless fragments of government bulletins." While it is doubtful whether Wang actually said this, it is true that Wang did not consider the book a particularly good history since it does not contain enough information. As to the moral principles that many Confucianists claimed to have derived from the judgments expressed in the *Ch'un-ch'iu*, they were often confused by none too reliable commentaries.[13]

The issue of the *Chou-li* versus the *Ch'un-ch'iu* involved far more than a mere dispute over the relative merits of the two sources or the reliability of certain commentaries upon them. Respect for the principles in the *Chou-li* leads toward the theory of an assertive government which should establish various systems to regulate the life of the people toward the realization of a moral society. What are these regulatory systems? If we permit ourselves the liberty of using modern social science terms, they are institutions, primarily government institutions to control the bureaucrats and government-initiated institutions to mold the behavioral pattern of the people. Wang definitely looked upon the institutional or external control of man's moral life as being more effective, if not more important, than moral self-cultivation, the personal or internal control of the individual. It was for this reason that he made changes in the political institutions his primary objective, although his ultimate goal was still the Confucian ideal of a moral society in which ethical values would be fully realized. In this sense he was an institutional reformer, but still within the Confucian tradition.

In contrast, the conservatives believed that the existing political institutions, though admittedly in need of some minor improvements, were on the whole tolerably satisfactory. Mere organization of the bureaucracy would not particularly help the political system. Neither could the government strengthen the economy by undue interference, nor could it improve social custom by legislation. To the conservatives, the need was not to change the political institutions, but to make them work better. Their reliance upon the *Ch'un-ch'iu* indicates a political theory of an ideal government by moral control over political behavior. With self-discipline, the worthy individuals would perform their government duties in the spirit of self-realization. Their self-realization, expressed through sound political measures and economic policies, would raise the moral standard of the people and of the social customs. Hence, the principle of government by moral leadership, example, and influence is the true path leading toward the ideal of a moral society. In short, the conservatives were the self-realizationists who upheld ethical considerations from beginning to end.

The controversy over the *Chou-li* and the *Ch'un-ch'iu* led to the second theoretical issue between the two groups, that of the nature of true statesmanship. The reformers regarded statesmanship, as had Ou-yang Hsiu, as the able management of state affairs (*ching-lun*) in accordance with the Confucian principles. They valued maximal utilitarian effectiveness within the bounds of moral scruples. The conservatives considered this a perversion. To them the essential principle of statesmanship lay in the "rectification of names" (*cheng-ming*). Name implied status: the rectification of names meant a strict observance of all relationships in the manner befitting the status of the parties involved. Without the rectification of names there would be a lack of moral behavior and moral order in the political system, and any able management of state affairs would tend to take the form of expediency in response to exigency, rather than of proper statesmanship.

The third and last theoretical issue concerned the book *Mencius*. Whether this book should be honored as a Confucian classic of prime importance was a question on which many scholars had often differed from the T'ang period on. By the time of Wang this question had become related to the two preceding issues in the controversy between the reformers and the conservatives. The reformers respected Mencius as a philosopher who saw the need to revive the ancient ideal systems of Chou, thereby improving upon the existing institutions, and who emphasized the role of the government in securing the economic welfare of the people, which no statesman should neglect. It is interesting that, long after these reformers, Chu Hsi in the Southern Sung period also honored Mencius, but for quite different reasons. Chu Hsi pointed out that Mencius really emphasized righteousness (*i*) far more than utilitarian advantages (*li*). Probably this interpretation is nearer to the truth and the reformers in this case were reading *Mencius* in terms of their own inclination. On the other hand, the conservatives, following Li Kou in this instance, cast doubt upon the *Mencius* as a deviant view within the Confucian heritage and as probably containing many distortions attributable to the disciples of the philosopher. This deviance and the alleged distortions caused the *Mencius* to display a lack of firmness in adhering to strict moral judgment and the principle of proper status, thus condoning a certain amount of expediency.[14]

The political theories of the reformers and the conservatives differed not only because they disagreed on the sources, the doctrines and the interpretations within Confucianism, but also because of other differences in their respective backgrounds. Differences in religious background probably had some bearing upon their divergent outlooks in political theory. Taoism was fairly strong in the north. Taoist astrological divination bore a close affinity to the study of the Book of Changes. The merging of Taoism and Confucianism was evident in the philosophy of Shao Yung (1011–1077), whom the conservatives held in great respect, and it was also noticeable in the thought of Ssu-ma Kuang, the leader at the beginning of the antireform phase.[15] The spirit of Taoism might have been one of the factors that led the conservatives to object to assertive government policies and their interference with the accustomed way of life.

Buddhism, on the other hand, after its decline in the north during the pre-Sung chaos, retained its strength mainly in the south. Its leading organizational centers were mostly in southern cities, with the exception of K'ai-feng, the national capital.[16] The reformers, being from the south, were probably influenced more by Buddhism than by Taoism. This was true in Wang's case. The opinion among scholars heretofore has been that Wang turned to Buddhism in his deep grief over his son's death and especially after his own retirement from politics, when he compiled his book on etymology by borrowing numerous Buddhist concepts.[17] However, during Wang's youth he and his family often stayed overnight in Buddhist temples on their visits to ancestral graves, and Wang himself in the prime of his life befriended several learned monks. In fact his belief in Buddhism was sufficiently strong for him to state openly in the court that the Buddhist or the Boddhisattva ideal of service to humanity coincided in some ways with the Confucian ideal.[18] In retirement Wang continued to discuss Buddhism in his correspondence with a former associate, Lü Hui-ch'ing, though in the meantime they had parted company politically.[19] He gave his property in Nanking to a Buddhist temple,[20] and he sent the Emperor two Buddhist scriptures.[21]

As often noted, Wang wrote many poems akin in spirit and style to Ch'an (or Zen) literature. He was sometimes credited with the introduction of Buddhist colloquialism into classical poetry, just as Su Shih was. The most famous of Wang's poems are twenty entitled "Casual Inspirations on a Cold Mountain," the second of which has been translated by Williamson. Perhaps a more striking example of Wang's Buddhist inclination and colloquial expression is the first half of number nine in this group:

> Having one is to have two,
> Having three is to have four.
> One, two, three, four, and five,
> Having them all, what does it really matter?

Two other poems suggest a strong Mahayana spirit. One, entitled "On the Wall of Pan-shan [halfway up the mountain] Temple — Number two," reads:

> When cold, sit in a warm place;
> When hot, walk in a cool place.
> All mortals are not different from Buddha.
> Buddha is all mortals.

Another, entitled "Dream," is even more revealing of Mahayana Buddhist influence:

Knowing that the world is like a dream makes one desire nothing.
When the heart desires nothing, the universe is void and still.
Yet, as in a dream, one might follow the circumstances of his
   dream,
And achieve millions and millions of dreamlike merits.

From these and a number of similar poems in his collected
works,[22] Wang appears as one who, having seen through
worldly affairs, turned not away from the world but toward
it, with a selfless fortitude, detached but compassionate, characteristic of the Mahayana teachings. This discussion does
not purport to show a strong tie between Buddhist influence
and the political thought of the reformers. Obviously, Buddhist
influence was by no means absent in the case of either the
northern conservatives or the southwestern moderates, whereas
it may have been negligible in the case of some reformers
other than Wang. The discussion merely suggests that between the Taoist spirit of quietude and resistance to disturbance with the natural or the accustomed way of life, on the
one hand, and the Buddhist spirit of compassion and service
to the humanity, on the other, the latter was more likely to
be adopted by the reformers, for it was more in accord with
their political theories.

The reformers and the conservatives also differed in socio-
political background. Toward the middle of the Northern
Sung period, the degree-holders and the high officials from
the south began to outnumber those from the north.[23] The
reformers, who were from the south and were relatively recent
arrivals upon the political scene, seemed noticeably eager to
exercise and even to augment their newly gained power. They
tended, as the research of Nieh and Sogabe reveals, to advocate measures of greater centralization and, at the same
time, more delegation of government authority to the officials. The conservatives, in principle though not necessarily

in actual practice, were opposed to such trends and openly accused the reformers of usurping power.[24] The southern reformers, as indicated by the research of Sudō and Aoyama Sadao, usually came from families of comparatively recent bureaucratic prominence.[25] As the new blood in the bureaucracy, they had a tendency to introduce innovations. The northern conservatives, whose families, relatives, and friends had long been associated with the government, probably felt more comfortable with the established pattern of bureaucratic behavior.

The reformers and the conservatives were probably set further apart by other differences in economic background. First, the factor of landownership was doubtless significant. The reformers represented principally the newly risen medium-sized landowners and the officials who had come from such landowning families but had since become professional bureaucrats, in the sense that their immediate families no longer owned a great deal of land and their major source of income was now their government salary. This was Wang's family background. It was only a few generations before him that his family had become prosperous enough to rise from the status of self-cultivators to the status of landowners. Wang's father, however, abandoned his native domicile. Either because his father had left little or no land, or because his immediate family, residing in Nanking after his father's death, had lived far beyond whatever income they had from their land, Wang complained that they had to depend entirely on his government salary.[26] Though the Wang family now qualified less as medium-sized landowners than as a family of professional bureaucrats, they still maintained their original socio-economic status and had cordial relations with families of similar origin in their native area.[27] On the other hand, the conservatives, according to Sudō's work on the

land system, represented essentially the interests of the heredi-
tary large landowners in the north. This probably explains
why such reform measures as the Land Survey and Equitable
Tax were initially applied to the northern areas, where many
large landowners indulged in tax evasion, and why these
measures met with strenuous opposition from the northern
conservatives.[28]

A second significant economic factor was the continuing
growth of the money economy. As the use of money was more
developed in the south,[29] it was more likely to influence the
thinking of reformers there. A knowledge and appreciation of
money economy evidently lent support to such policies as the
expansion of state financing, loans to the landowners and
farmers, and the engagement of the state in trading activities.
It was no mere coincidence that two of Wang's close associates, Lü Hui-Ch'ing and Ts'ai Ch'üeh (1036–1093), who
were most active in formulating and executing these policies,
both came from the famous trading port of Ch'üan-chou,
known in early Western literature as Zayton, on the southern
Fukien coast. From the research of Sogabe, Ch'üan Han-
sheng, and others, we see that among the major economic
results of the reform phase were: first, heavy taxation, increased revenues, and a treasury surplus;[30] second, a moderate
expansion in the volume of currency, as a great deal of the
increased issue of currency found its way back to the government in the form of revenues; and third, a deflationary fall
in prices as the inflationary tendency of the moderate increase
in currency circulation was more than compensated by good
harvests.[31] These circumstances, added to the fact that the
state itself engaged in several trading activities, were dis-
advantageous to the merchants, who probably earned less than
they would have earned without the reforms.[32]

The conservatives on their part responded negatively to

money economy. They opposed the expanding state finance and the state's involvement in trading activities not only on the policy level but also on the theoretical level, denouncing such operations as profit-seeking in violation of Confucianism.[33] Yet the opposition was probably not entirely free from selfish interest. Ch'üan has shown the connection between some conservative officials, whose families had long resided in the capital of K'ai-feng, and the merchants there.[34] Thus the opposition may have reflected the objections of the merchants when features of the money economy that were introduced into the state policy cut into their profits.

In any event, their differences in economic background are plausible explanations of why the reformers favored active government participation in both the land economy and the money economy, whereas the conservatives favored leaving the economic system largely in the hands of the landowners and the merchants as before. However, in the present state of research, conclusions as to the relation of these various background factors to the differences in political theory between the reformers and the conservatives can be no more than hypotheses. These hypotheses are offered in the hope that they may stimulate further study.

WANG'S POLITICAL AND ECONOMIC THEORIES

To avoid undue repetition of what is available in the previous works on Wang and in such other well-known sources as Hsiao's general history of Chinese political thought, this discussion will be limited to a summary, under several salient topics, of Wang's political and economic theories.

On human nature and social custom. As the philosophical

basis of his political thought, Wang held that human nature (*hsing*), not being good or evil in itself, is inseparably bound to human emotions (*ch'ing*). In his own words:

Human nature is the substance of human emotions and human emotions are the functioning of human nature. This is why I maintain that the two are really mingled as one . . . . The worthy man cultivates the goodness of nature and his emotions become good. The unworthy ones indulge in the evilness of nature and their emotions likewise become bad.[35]

The development of human nature and the taming of emotions depend a great deal on social custom (*feng-su*), which exercises the institutional control necessary for a moral life. Wang said:

The sages rule the people in accordance with the wishes of Heaven. The main task is to give the people security and wealth. The essence of this task is none other than the rectification of social customs. Changes in social customs affect the volition of the people on which the prosperity or decadence of the country depends.[36]

Wang believed that all social customs are in a sense restraints imposed upon the people and the rules of proper behavior or propriety (*li*) are not an exception. The rules of proper behavior are nevertheless in basic accord with human nature and human desires. Hence, the ancient philosopher Hsün-tzu is wrong in this respect:

Hsün-tzu contends that the sages use the rules of proper behavior to reform human nature in order to remove the evil in it. He is mistaken because he does not understand that the rules of proper behavior have their origins in Heaven. . . . Men are born with the inclination to respect a strict father and a loving mother. The sages, in following this inclination of human nature, formulate the rules to regulate men's behavior further. Though the rules of behavior seem to be restraints imposed upon the people, they respond basically to what human nature desires.[37]

Social custom and the rule of the government. Moral teachings and influence, Wang believed, are important. "They can improve social customs; however, they take a long time to attain the desired objective." [38] Wang, in differing with the moralistic conservatives, advocated that the government should play its part in the molding of society through "regulatory systems (*fa-tu*), codes (*hsing*), and government policies (*cheng*)." The compound *fa-tu* literally means "laws and measures," but its general meaning is "that which governs and regulates." Hence, it may be translated as regulatory systems established by the government which have the function of institutional control over behavior. Wang continued:

The ways of the ancient kings that can be transmitted to the succeeding generations in words and that can be put into effect with good results are the regulatory systems, the codes, and the government policies, rather than the function (*yung*) of their spiritual enlightenment (*shen-ming*).[39]

Wang held the conviction that the government can rule the country well by setting up and strengthening institutional controls of various kinds:

When a worthy man governs, he establishes good systems (*fa*) for the country and the country becomes well administered . . . . As the Duke of Chou understood how, he would rely upon a school system for the country to get the talents, rather than [as Hsün-tzu erroneously alleges] exerting himself in welcoming the talented people of the country. Such exertion could have no more than limited results. It would also be impractical in many circumstances.[40]

Wang believed that the government failed to play its part in improving the social customs, as the principles laid down by the sagacious rulers in ancient times required it to do. He argued this same point in two separate memorials:

The government now has strict laws (*fa*) and numerous orders (*ling*), as complete as they can be. Yet your humble servant thinks that the government does not have good laws and measures, that is, regulatory systems (*fa-tu*). This is because many existing systems fail to agree with the government policies (*cheng*) of the ancient kings.[41]

According to Wang, the *Chou-li* offered the best example of regulatory systems instituted by the government:

The scholars have long been handicapped by conventional learning. In kind consideration, His Majesty desires their improvement through the proper study of the classics . . . . The best time in history was the reign of Ch'eng-wang in the Chou dynasty. Its regulating systems, that which can be applied to the succeeding generations, and its records, that which is transmitted in words, are mostly found in *Chou-li*.[42]

However, the time element had to be taken into consideration. It would be a mistake to imitate the ancient systems mechanically without due adaptation to the circumstances of the present. What the government should do was to devise new systems in the same spirit and with the same objective of improving social custom:

Some people nowadays, without much clear thinking, want to follow the exact footsteps of the ancient kings. They do not understand the necessity of weighing the time element in making changes for the present. To have the same ancient form would actually result in a different substance . . . . Nothing will cause more harm to the country than having the same form but actually a different substance.[43]

What the country now needed was "to change the present systems without losing the substance of the ancient principles." This, Wang maintained, was "what those officials who have mastered the principles are capable of doing." [44]

On utilitarian policies. Wang believed that the ancient sages attached great value not only to moral behavior but also to useful results. He said:

What the spirit can do, even when it reaches the highest stage, cannot be seen by the world. The spirit produces observable results only when it manifests itself in compassion (*jen*) and when it expresses itself in application (*yung*). The spirit is the means by which the sages purify their minds, in seclusion and privacy. But it is also the means by which the sages extend their compassion to give ceaseless help to everything useful in the world and to exert their influence, without ever wearying, on what can be applied to thousands of generations. This is what makes them sages.[45]

Attaching importance to useful social results should not be confused with following the expedient "way of hegemony" (*pa*). On the other hand, the moral "way of the ideal king" (*wang*) by no means excludes practical considerations. Wang considered the "way of the ideal king" to be fundamentally as utilitarian as it was moral. He said:

The way of the ideal king relies on utmost sincerity to seek benefits (or profits, *li*). And the world follows it. Even when it does not deliberately so seek, it will accumulate benefits just the same.[46]

Believing in a utilitarian orientation for government policies, Wang objected to the mere study of and overemphasis upon the commentaries on the classics, metaphysics, and literary formalism.[47] A famous poet himself, he regretted the time he had spent on the compilation of an anthology of T'ang poetry.[48] Nor did he confine his studies and inquiries to Confucian literature. As he explained:

The complete texts of the classics have been lost to the world for a long time. Mere study of the classics [in their incomplete form] cannot therefore really enable one to understand them fully. I have read the works of various philosophers in a hundred different schools, and even the medical books like *Nan-ching, Su-wen* and *Pen-ts'ao,* as well as the novels. Indeed, I have not even neglected to ask for information from farmers and female servants.[49]

This passage shows what a broad-minded scholar Wang was and how he tried to link Confucian principles with their application to practical problems.

On law and bureaucracy. Wang emphasized law a great deal more than the conservative Confucianists did. It can be said that Wang's thought was closer to the Legalist theories than that of most Confucianists. However, Wang's basic emphasis was neither on law, nor on the Legalist belief in punishment and reward as the means to achieve good government. His famous "myriad word memorial" continually stresses the fundamental importance of capable officials, how to train (*chiao*) them, how to cultivate (*yang*) them by paying them well, by restraining them according to the rules of proper behavior and by controlling them with law, how to select (*chü*) the best among them, and how to entrust (*jen*) the best ones with a larger measure of executive power.[50]

This memorial is a remarkable document outlining a kind of bureaucratic idealism. By bureaucratic idealism we mean a political view that upholds the ideal of a professionally well-trained and administratively well-controlled bureaucracy as the principal instrument in striving toward the realization of Confucian moral society. There should be good government institutions to guide the behavior of the bureaucrats and there should also be good government-initiated institutions to control and to mold the behavior of the people.

On the question of law, Ch'ü T'ung-tsu has shown that all Confucianists since the Han period accepted the necessity for law and differed only in their interpretations of the proper function of law and in their degrees of emphasis.[51] And the research of Saeki Tomi shows that the law during the Sung was more severe than that of the preceding T'ang period. Furthermore, the Sung government, in an effort to enforce order in certain strategic, sensitive, or troubled areas, designated them "heavy penalty areas" and in these areas it imposed heavier penalties than on the same crimes committed elsewhere.[52] It is, consequently, not surprising that Wang and many other Sung Confucianists should have considered law more important than their predecessors did. However, Wang did not see how reliance on law alone could lead to good government:

> To emphasize penalizing will make the penalties heavy. But the country will become less well governed. Not to rely on penalizing will make the penalties light. Yet the country will be much better governed.[53]

As a Confucianist Wang repeatedly upheld the dictum that law does not administer itself. As a bureaucratic idealist within Confucianism, he attached far greater importance to the administrator. The ultimate aim of good government was the moral education of the people. In terms of this aim, Wang did not believe that law would be very helpful:

> Someone may ask, are the laws (fa), the orders (ling), the imperial commandments (kao), and the official injunctions (chieh) inadequate to educate the people? My answer is that they are mere words. What I emphasize is the principle of education. I

do not understand how it could be possible to neglect the principle and to rely on words.[54]

However, by the principle of education Wang, unlike his conservative opponents, did not mean the principle of moral teachings alone. Individual self-cultivation and self-realization were desirable but were not sufficiently effective. In the principle of education Wang definitely included regulatory systems to promote the moral behavior of the people.

On the functions of the bureaucrats. There is little doubt that in Wang's mind improvement of the bureaucracy was the crucial task in statecraft. But his standards for desirable bureaucrats were quite different from those upheld by the conservatives, who emphasized moral qualities. His view was:

Before the regulatory systems (*fa-tu*) of the country are established, it is imperative to search for and make use of the talented men who are capable of reviving the regulatory systems of the ancient kings.[55]

In another passage, he said:

To improve the system (*fa*) and to select good officials to administer it so that the finance of the country can be better managed is a task of such utmost urgency that even Emperor Yao or Emperor Shun could not possibly overlook it.[56]

The major faults of the bureaucrats, Wang felt, were their craving for fame and their lack of both utilitarian orientation and practical ability.[57] The preparation of scholars and the emphases of the state examinations lay in a wrong direction:

The examination of the doctoral candidates merely emphasizes the formal style and the rules of rhymes. Lesser talents can master all that. The examination on the classics sets a premium on memorization and fails to ask questions on the interpretation of their deep meanings. Even the unenlightened ones can pass it. On the other hand, the talented candidates who understand a great deal of the world may not be favored by the present standard. The scholars who are much ahead of society may suffer from discrimination because of the prevailing conventional ideas.[58]

What Wang wanted was bureaucrats who excelled in the interpretation of the classics, in adapting the classics to the active roles of the government, in policy deliberations, in administrative ability, and in knowledge of the law. The multiple functions of the government required these qualifications.

Wang was convinced that the government should expand its activities, which would require a correspondingly enlarged bureaucracy. A very striking statement of his conviction is the following:

Only with many officials can the numerous tasks be accomplished. So long as the tasks are done, there is nothing wrong in having many activities. Large expenditures will bring about increasing prosperity. So long as they help prosperity, there is no harm in more allotments of funds.[59]

On state finance. The above passage and a number of others in Wang's writings conclusively show that he gave a great deal of thought to state finance. Successful finance, it is relevant to recall, was a definite, though minor, concern in the Confucian heritage. The notable exponents of this minor concern were Sang Hung-yang (143–80 B.C.) and Liu Yen (A.D. 715–780). The former was sometimes considered a Legalist, though the latter, with a policy which effectively responded to the rise of money economy during the T'ang period, was rarely so criticized.[60] In fact, successful financing had received attention from a number of prominent Sung statesmen before Wang, for instance Fan Chung-yen, who led the first reform of 1043–1044.[61] What was remarkable about

Wang was his new or unconventional Confucian theory on finance. He believed that:

To hold together the people in the country is impossible without finance; to manage the finance of the country without righteousness (*i*) . . . and to weigh the decisions on revenues and expenditures is impossible without knowing the techniques (*shu*).[62]

Good financing requires not only measures of economy, as the conventional Confucianists always advocated, but also positive steps to increase the state revenues, the productivity of the country and the wealth of the people. In Wang's own words:

The deficit of the government nowadays is not due to excessive expenditures alone, but also to the lack of ways to increase incomes. Those who wish to enrich their families merely take from the state; those who wish to enrich the state merely take from the country; and those who wish to enrich the country merely take from natural resources. The case is analogous to that of a family in which no effort is being made for the son to increase his income, but the demanding father merely takes from him. Though the family hopes to become more wealthy, it never will be, for there are only transactions behind the closed doors of the family, with nothing coming in from the outside. Even when the father takes everything that the son has, the family does not get any richer. Discussions of financial benefits (*li*) in recent times, though good, are all limited to the techniques (*shu*) of how the state can take from the country. These are precisely the techniques of making transactions within the same household. And this is the reason why the state finance has become so strained.[63]

In other words, Wang did not believe that the state should bear down hard upon the people. The state could increase its revenues best by helping the people to become more productive. What the state needed, therefore, was a system of expanding finance that enlarged both the scope and the amount of government financing to stimulate and facilitate economic growth, so that the state would ultimately derive a larger share for itself from increased productivity and a greater measure of general prosperity. Wang said:

If the state improves its institutions (*fa-tu*) so as to make the [productive] base grow strong and the [consumer] end diminish, then the wealth of the country will be so great that no matter how much the state uses it cannot possibly exhaust all of it.[64]

This emphasis upon state finance, according to Wang, by no means conflicted with Confucian principles, for "many government policies are concerned with the management of finance, and the management of finance aims precisely at what is meant by righteousness (*i*)."[65] Ssu-ma Kuang charged that the New Policies sought benefits or profits (*li*), the very opposite of righteousness. Wang retorted, "managing the finance for the whole country can in no sense be equated with making profits."[66]

The conventional Confucian theory rested on the economic assumption that if the government spent less, the people would have more for themselves. This would be true in a static economy. Wang made a contrary economic assumption that, if the government took the initiative in stimulating productivity, even though it spent far more than before, the people would still have more for themselves. This would be true in a dynamic economy.

On land economy and trade. Wang may be regarded as a physiocrat, as all Confucianists were apt to be, in emphasizing irrigation, in promoting agricultural productivity, and also in favoring a heavier burden of taxation on the merchants, rather than the farmers.[67] But he went one step further than many other Confucianists. Reflecting his own socio-economic background, he was hostile toward the concentration of land-ownership and of money in the hands of a few who exploited the farmers.[68] This was part of his reason for introducing the State Farming Loans so that the farmers could keep their land without having to borrow from the moneylenders. On the other hand, Wang may be regarded as a sort of mercantilist in making the government become an active agent in trade, thus differing radically from the conservatives. Under the Tribute and Distribution System introduced by Wang, the government saved itself the trouble of transporting the revenues in kind from the places where the government received them to the places where it had use for them. Instead, the government simply sold in the market when and where its supply of revenue in kind exceeded its own local demand and bought from the market when and where its demand exceeded its local supply. Thus, under another reform measure, the State Trade System, a special government agency was established to buy other supplies directly from the small merchants. Both these systems had a twofold purpose: to improve the state finance and to stabilize the market price. Wang was evidently interested in achieving an economy that was expanding and yet stable. Stable prices were to the interest of consumers, and the state itself was a large consumer, since it had to use its revenues in cash to buy the supplies not provided by its revenue in kind. Stable prices were also to the interest of bureaucrats like Wang himself, who were consumers living on salary incomes, rather than producers.

Wang did not favor government control or intervention in all trades, precisely because of this consumers' standpoint. For example, he opposed the state control of tea because it imposed a number of administrative difficulties upon the government; moreover, while it hurt the large tea merchants (many of whom, incidentally, were from Wang's native area), the consumers in the end had to pay a higher price for tea of inferior quality.[69]

Wang's theory on expanding state finance led him to formulate these policies on land economy and trade. Inasmuch as his thought remained largely anchored to the Confucian philosophy, he failed to develop operational economic theories that dealt directly with many specific economic activities. In fact, he frequently depended upon the advice of his associates who were more familiar with the actual economic conditions.

WANG'S THEORIES IN ACTION

Wang had the rare opportunity, enjoyed by few statesmen in history, of putting many of his ideas into actual practice. For he enjoyed the almost unreserved trust of the Emperor from the beginning of the reform in 1069 to the time of his temporary resignation from the court in 1074.[70] The only political opposition that disturbed him was the incessant criticism of the censors, and these, on the insistence of Wang, were demoted one after another.[71]

The improvement of custom by government initiative. The task Wang defined for himself was fourfold: "the production of well-trained personnel, the further improvement of state finance, the change to better customs, and the issuance of better orders and laws." [72] The most fundamental of these was the improvement of custom through the regulatory systems to be instituted by the government. Wang repeatedly used the expression "custom" (*feng-su*) as a keynote in discussing policies with the Emperor, and the Emperor, evidently under his influence, did the same.[73] However, there is evident in his writings a crucial change in the meaning of the word "custom." In the writings before he assumed power, the term referred to social custom in general. In his discussions at the court, it referred principally to the practices and political behavior among the bureaucrats, or in other words, the "political custom" of the bureaucracy in particular. Among his numerous comments to the Emperor, the following two are especially revealing. On one occasion Wang commented on the prevailing practices and attitudes of the bureaucrats:

The worst defect in the present practices is the lack of loyalty (*chung*) and honesty (*hsin*) and the disregard of financial integrity (*lien*) and sense of honor (*ch'ih*). A man like Ch'ang Chih conducts himself admirably and should be praised and honored. To keep him at the court helps to set a good example and promote good practices.[74]

This comment was in perfect accord with the belief of the conservatives. But Wang did not mean to stop there. On another occasion he discussed the relative importance of improving practices among the bureaucrats and "enriching the state and strengthening the army." He came to the conclusion that they were equally important:

What Wu Ch'i [of the Warring Kingdom Period] did in enriching the state and strengthening the army is naturally not the way of virtuous men (*chün-tzu*). . . . The ancient kings, having improved upon their government policies and made their state sufficiently strong, took steps to perfect the customs so that their descendants, even when faced with the hardship of poverty or the crisis of disruption in the succession to the throne, would have no rebellious disturbance. To make no effort to promote loyalty, honesty, financial integrity and sense of honor, but to concentrate on strengthening the state — that was the failure of the Ch'in empire. On the other hand, to make no effort to improve upon the government policies, but to concentrate on rewarding those who were chaste, righteous, financially clean and admirably modest

—that was the failure of the late Han empire. In both cases, the mistake was to lean toward the one, neglecting the other.[75]

Wang's opinion is quite clear. The utilitarian policies are the immediate tasks; but moral improvement remains, as all Confucianists believe, the ultimate goal. Both are necessary conditions of good government; neither is sufficient in itself. As a matter of fact, Wang kept on reminding the Emperor that, in spite of all the New Policies already introduced, one fundamental reform was yet to be carried out, namely a change toward higher standards of conduct.[76]

Regulatory systems and laws. Wang differed from his conservative opponents in yet another important respect. It was his conviction that the desired change toward higher standards of conduct could not be achieved by moral education alone. It would require an improvement in popular custom which must be regulated by more effective institutional controls. The government should participate actively in setting up various regulatory systems and in promulgating good laws. This was exactly what the ancient sagacious emperors had done, and it should not be confused at all with the emphasis upon mere laws or mainly upon rewards and punishments that was peculiar to the Legalists.[77] In fact, judging from the government activities under Wang it is more correct to say that the reform stressed the need for better administrative systems more than the need for effective laws. During the reform phase, the government accounting system was revised and 400 fascicles of the rules and regulations of the Finance Commission were compiled.[78] Officials were appointed to study administrative procedures and problems.[79] The government also ordered a new codification of the laws and the decrees, but this was not regarded as particularly important.[80]

With regard to the application of the laws, Wang himself considered the codes too severe and the use of capital punishment excessive.[81] It cannot be denied that in the promotion of the reform measures many violators were frequently penalized by law. But this is attributable more to the officials foregoing the usual means of nonlegal suasion, rather than to the New Policies or their intention.[82] It should also be noted that after Wang's first resignation Lü Hui-ch'ing, who succeeded him, hardly discussed the long-range objective of promoting better practices and good social customs. Lü did not even introduce further changes in the administrative system but directed his attention mainly to administrative measures and laws.[83]

The classification of Wang as a Legalist was a matter of opinion. Some of his opponents compared him to Wang Mang, the usurper and reformer of the Han period who deviated from Confucianism through his incorrect interpretation of the *Chou-li*. Other opponents regarded Wang An-shih as no less than a Legalist who followed the teachings of Han-fei-tzu and the policies of Shang Yang of the Ch'in kingdom in "enriching the state and strengthening the army."[84] However, these were minority opinions at the time. The strongest attacks upon Wang and the reform were directed toward the state financing policies as profit-seeking operations, undertaken by profit-minded and unscrupulous officials in defiance of general opinion, and causing great disturbance and suffering among the common people. Many opponents, like Ssu-ma Kuang, still recognized Wang as a Confucianist, though a misguided one, rather than as a Legalist.

It was the Southern Sung scholars who later reached the conclusion that Wang was either a Legalist in disguise or came rather close to being one.[85] Even then, the philosopher Chu Hsi, who was not altogether favorable to the New

Policies, dissented.[86] By this time the crux of the problem lay in a definition of terms. Some of Wang's critics alleged that the word *fa* and the expression *fa-tu*, which Wang used frequently, essentially meant law, or law and measures, and therefore Wang should be classified as a Legalist. Yet, when numerous passages either in Wang's writings or in his oral comments are examined closely in their context, it is hard thus to restrict the meaning of the word *fa* and the expression *fa-tu* to this specific sense. The more inclusive rendering of "regulatory systems" is probably closer to Wang's real meaning.

Enriching the state and strengthening the army. Confucius himself advocated sufficient food for the people and sufficient defense of the state. Toward the end of the nineteenth century, a number of Confucianists also emphasized these needs. However, according to most, if not all, Confucianists, the Legalists were those who overemphasized the desirability of "enriching the state and strengthening the army" and who sought to attain this objective by expediency instead of through moralistic policies. The question here is whether or not Wang in actual administration did move in the Legalist direction. Wang was in favor of enriching the state through various financial measures.[87] According to his concept of expanding finance, government spending to promote general economic growth would in turn bring into the treasury revenues in excess of expenditures; "there need be no worry of fund shortage" at all.[88] Under the New Policies the state acquired surplus funds and used them to finance additional activities. The cardinal objective of Wang's financial policy was neither the welfare of the farmers nor the elimination of monopolistic trade interests, but the financial security of the state itself.[89] Wang assumed that the state was the organized body ideally representing the totality of the country. Its interests therefore would come before the interests of the common people as individuals.

However important it was to enrich the state, this task, to Wang, was only one among many. The reform of the bureaucracy in order to insure a better administration of all measures, and the improvement of custom through moral influence were of more basic importance and should never be neglected. Unfortunately, the circumstances were such that Wang was unable to make much progress toward these long-range goals. Among other reasons, the Emperor exerted considerable pressure on Wang to give primary attention to the urgent problem of state finance, first to wipe out the deficit and then to meet the increasing demand for funds.[90] Wang probably did overemphasize the objective of enriching the state, but not entirely of his own choice.

On strengthening the army, the Emperor and Wang clearly differed. It was always the Emperor who brought military affairs and strategy up for discussion. He was quite sensitive about the military weakness of his empire and rather anxious to have this situation remedied.[91] Wang agreed to the desirability of territorial expansion at the expense of minority groups in the west, in the south, and in the southwest. But he was opposed to attacking either the Hsi Hsia kingdom on the northwest or the Liao empire on the north. On many occasions when the Emperor initiated a discussion of the army, Wang countered with the advice that financial strength must come before military strength and internal reform before external expansion.[92]

The *pao-chia* policing system, though highly significant, was not as important to the government policy at the time as is sometimes believed; nor was it exactly the forerunner of a conscription system, as some interpretations maintain. It was originally introduced for the prime purpose of maintaining local order and of protecting property rights. When organized, the *pao-chia* policing system also facilitated census taking and tax collection, and helped to eliminate tax evasion. The use of *pao-chia* units as reserve forces in time of war came later, and this never did become their dominant function.[93] In short, Wang was far more in favor of enriching the state than of strengthening the army. And neither was nearly as important to Wang as the reform of the bureaucracy, and the effort of the bureaucracy to set up regulatory systems that would ultimately promote better social customs. In action Wang remained largely true to his theories, which we have described as expressive of a sort of idealism — hoping to use a well-organized bureaucracy for the realization of a moral society.

IV

The New Policies and the Behavior of the Bureaucrats

BUREAUCRATIC PRACTICES BELOW THE CONFUCIAN STANDARDS

Although Wang emphasized the primary need for a reformed bureaucracy, on which the success of all other reform measures essentially depended, he was not the only one to see this need. It was a well-known fact that many bureaucratic practices tended to fall below the Confucian standards. Paradoxically, however, Wang's efforts to improve bureaucratic behavior met with limited and dubious success. On the other hand, the old illness was compounded by new complications. The behavior of many bureaucrats became increasingly difficult to control. The reality of a large bureaucracy, bitterly divided and with a low morale, betrayed the fatal weakness of Wang's theory of bureaucratic idealism. Under these circumstances, the New Policies could not possibly succeed or endure.

Although the Sung civil service on the whole maintained fairly high standards, the bureaucracy, as Miyazaki has shown, was nevertheless laden with corruption and political maneuvering.[1] The official income of the bureaucrats was higher in the Sung than in previous dynasties. Though the local government officials got far less than those in the capital, their complaints led to some increase in the allotment of office land, the rent from which was a part of their emolument.[2] However, those who did not come from wealthy families or did not have private means often found their incomes inadequate to meet the rising prices and the rising standard of an urban mode of living.[3] Su Shih outspokenly expressed the opinion that the inability of bureaucrats to enjoy a gracious living was something that should not have happened in a peaceful and prosperous reign.[4] Wang was not unsympathetic to the same sentiment. During the reform phase the officials were given an increase in salary. Evidently Wang introduced this measure in the hope that it would raise morale and reduce corruption among the bureaucrats. While he was in power, an appreciable improvement did take place,[5] but soon afterward the increase was offset by the rise of prices during the antireform phase and especially by the inflation under the postreform maladministration.[6] Whatever Wang's policy had accomplished was again lost.

Unscrupulous bureaucrats, dissatisfied with their official income, turned to corruption. This became noticeable as early as the reign of Chen-tsung.[7] Corruption took many forms. A mild form was for the bureaucrats to use the office expense funds and requisition provisions from the service personnel for their private social occasions. A party, usually with entertainers, often cost some twenty to thirty thousand coins.[8] Sometimes the bureaucrats would raise a loan from local wealthy families by leaving the office silverware in pawn.[9] Another form of corruption was the engaging in trade through abuse of the bureaucratic privilege of exemption from inspection. Su Shih, for example, was censored for shipping salt, lumber, and chinaware while on home leave for his father's funeral.[10] A more serious form of corruption, pointed out by Ch'üan, was trading regularly either with private funds or using office funds, relying on official prestige or on corrupt cooperation with merchants.[11] There were, of course, far worse corruptions, such as embezzlement and falsification of office accounts, obtaining thousands of silver pieces illegally from the people by conspiring with large local landlords, and taking over by pressure the properties of other people.[12] Such poor practices, with their disregard of the Confucian standards, probably offer one explanation of why the families of some officials in the south, who did not have much land at the beginning of the reform phase, eventually became large landowners toward the end of the Northern Sung period.[13] The most frank confession of bureaucratic abusiveness came from Teng Chien, a nominal but unworthy follower of the reform, who said, "Despise and curse me as much as you like, but I am going to enjoy this good office." [14]

Wang, an idealistic scholar-official, maintained high standards for himself. He lived a simple, frugal, and even reclusive life, showing the influence of the Buddhist ideals of self-discipline and renunciation.[15] While he favored increasing the salaries of the officials so that they would have enough income without indulging in financial dishonesty, he also reduced the office expense funds, much to the displeasure of the self-indulgent bureaucrats.[16] Wang's attack upon corruption, however, was not entirely free from partiality. He criticized such political opponents as Su Shih for their relatively minor misconduct, but in looking for followers with administrative ability, he often overlooked the possibility that they might misdirect their talents to enrich themselves.[17] In devoting his attention mainly to policy matters, Wang probably failed to watch a few individuals who managed to perform their official duties to his satisfaction while at the same time pursuing their selfish interests in an unscrupulous manner. After Wang's retirement the high standards were relaxed and corruption increased. By the time of the postreform, abusive

practices had become far worse than ever before. In this connection the conservatives were justified in blaming Wang for
not giving primary emphasis to the self-cultivation of moral
character and for opening the door of power to many unscrupulous bureaucrats.

Another practice below the Confucian standard was treacherous political maneuvering, which was excessive. It was accepted as normal behavior for bureaucrats to ingratiate themselves with leading officials and to be considered their retainers
or "guests at the door" (men-hsia-k'e). Some overzealous bureaucrats even courted the favor of the relatives and close
friends of those in power.[18] Others made daily calls to so many
private residences that they earned the nickname of "wander-
ing spirits." [19] Wang was critical of such activity. He refused
to receive those who came to congratulate him upon his assumption of office, accepted few social engagements, declined
to drink, and kept only a few chosen friends.[20] In this manner
he probably antagonized many bureaucrats. On the other
hand, Wang was frequently surrounded by his subordinates,
who discussed official business with him incessantly and thus
prevented others from getting close to him or from mention-
ing anything unfavorable about the reform.[21] Wang, who was
trying to reform the bureaucracy, thus become more and
more isolated from the majority of the bureaucrats.

Ingratiation was a minor fault compared with the ma-
nipulations of unprincipled bureaucrats in which idealistic
scholar-officials were often caught defenseless. For example,
the reform of Fan Chung-yen was undermined by the summary dismissal of several of his followers upon the accusation
that they had slandered the emperor at a drinking party.[22]
Wang, who had the confidence of the emperor, was nearly
immune from the possibility of such attacks. However, the
decisive turning point of his reform, as we have seen, was

his first resignation from the court in 1074, and a contributory cause of this fall from power was the maneuvering within his own camp, principally by Lü Hui-ch'ing. Tseng Pu, against Wang's wishes, verified by investigation that the State Trade System and the Guild Exemption Tax were faulty in execution. Wang, who had persistently defended these measures before the Emperor, felt humiliated. He assigned Lü, who stood by him, to make a further investigation, not without the hope of repairing the political damage. Lü used the investigation as a weapon to aggravate the discord between Wang and Tseng without, however, entirely exonerating Wang of policy error. Shortly thereafter Wang resigned and recommended Lü as his successor. As soon as Lü assumed power he demoted Tseng to a local government post, ceased to be friendly toward Wang, and attempted to draw other followers of Wang over to his side. But he was not long in power. When Wang returned the following year, the same kind of maneuvering on the part of lesser figures like Teng Chien helped to bring about the fall of Lü. The removal from responsible positions of Tseng and Lü, both experienced executives, shattered the unity of the reform group and left the execution of the New Policies in far less capable hands.[23]

There were frequent cases of similar treachery after Wang retired and again during the postreform. Lü relied upon Yang Wei, and Yang soon turned against him. Tseng Pu, when later he was reinstated, had to share power with Ts'ai Ching, and eventually Ts'ai not only removed Tseng from power but deliberately plotted a false accusation of corruption against him.[24] Maneuvers such as these were largely responsible for the disappearance of the reform zeal soon after Wang's fall from power and especially during the postreform.

For various reasons Wang's struggle against poor bureaucratic behavior was largely frustrated. Meanwhile, new complications arose. Wang gathered officials whom he believed to be professionally competent to devise and execute numerous New Policies. His aim was to reorganize the bureaucracy with a utilitarian orientation. In his efforts at recruitment and reorganization he was accused of favoritism and factionalism by his opponents.

In the Sung civil service, as a rule, promotions through routine procedure after a definite term of service with cumulative merits were much slower than promotions made upon the special recommendations of high-ranking officials. More often than not, such recommendations were based upon an honest evaluation of the candidates and upon the consensus in official circles. Nonetheless, a certain amount of favoritism inevitably existed. Wang's own rise to power provides a case in point. He was repeatedly recommended by several high-ranking officials, including a few on the conservative side and Ou-yang Hsiu, who was from the same province as Wang.[25] These recommendations were based mainly upon Wang's widespread reputation as an idealistic scholar who combined Confucian principles and utilitarian policies. Although his appointment was initially greeted with general acclaim, it was not entirely independent of personal connections. Han Wei, a former tutor of the emperor, at the time a prince, had praised Wang highly. Both the Han family and the Wang family were related by marriage to the family of Wu Ch'ung (1021–1080).[26]

As long as personal connections were not the chief reason for promotion, and more importantly, as long as the honest evaluations upon which the recommendations rested were in accord with the opinion prevailing among the majority of the officials, there could be no charge of favoritism. Wang was accused of favoritism in his personnel policy precisely because the prevailing majority opinion among the officials did not support his evaluation of those whom he recommended.

Through Wang's recommendation, Han Wei, his brother Han Chiang (1021–1088), and Wu Ch'ung all held high positions. Hsieh Ching-wen, another of Wang's relatives, was made a censor, and he helped Wang to bring about the demotion of Su Shih.[27] Furthermore, those who had studied under Wang and those who supported his political theories were given positions at the National Academy and prefectural schools.[28] These people in turn showed a marked partiality toward candidates of similar scholastic and political inclinations.[29] It was these facts that led Ssu-ma Kuang to accuse Wang of "drawing upon his own relatives and factional followers to monopolize key posts in the government." [30]

In all fairness, Wang's personnel policy was based upon partisanship rather than personal favoritism, although his opponents saw no distinction between the two. At the beginning of the reform Wang recommended a number of leading scholar-officials because they were held in public esteem. But many of them refused to cooperate with him. For example, Wang recommended Liu Chih, but the conservative Liu turned out to be one of Wang's severest critics.[31] As time went on, Wang expressed regret that many conservatives, like Lü Kung-chu, who had been friendly to him before he assumed power, now refused to join him or to support the reform.[32]

Wang did not necessarily prefer those with whom he was personally connected. For example, he dismissed his relative, Hsieh, when Hsieh disagreed with him on policy matters.[33] But he was promoting a program of drastic reforms which was opposed by the majority of the officials, and in these circumstances he had no choice but to rely increasingly on those who supported his policies. It was unfortunate, however, that such a reliance upon personnel made Wang more and more intolerant of critics and opponents. He once told the Emperor that he "would prefer the appointment of ordinary officials with no particular distinction to that of talented ones who would obstruct the government policy." [34]

Wang denied that he and his associates formed a faction. According to him, they cooperated because they had a meeting of minds.[35] In selecting personnel, Wang generally valued administrative ability and, occasionally, political skill.[36] But his opponents charged that Wang recommended only unscrupulous bureaucrats who knew how to make profits, either for the government, which was contrary to conventional Confucian ideas, or for themselves, which was even worse. This was an exaggeration. The studies on Wang by both Liang Ch'i-ch'ao and K'e Ch'ang-i prove that among Wang's subordinates there were many talented and honest officials.[37] Hsüeh Hsiang was an excellent and incorrupt financier.[38] Wang Shao proved to be a great general.[39] Only a few of Wang's followers were unscrupulous, and the appointment of these few was the result simply of misjudgment on Wang's part.

The whole issue of factionalism had arisen earlier during the reform of Fan Chung-yen.[40] From that time on, even when there was no particular controversy over policy, the bureaucrats tended to draw factional battlelines. A well-known instance occurred over a mere matter of ritual, when the question arose as to how Emperor Ying-tsung (reign: 1063–67) should honor the late prince P'u who had been his father. On this question Ou-yang Hsiu took one side and many northern conservatives took the other. It was the same group of northern conservatives that later opposed Wang.[41] They not only attacked the reform but also persisted in developing ritual matters into political issues or weapons of criticism. For example, Wang promoted Li Ting, and his opponents discovered that Li had failed to observe mourning for his mother.

The attack upon Li lasted several months, until a legal investigation ascertained the fact that, owing to the second
marriage of Li's mother long ago, Li had no way of knowing
at the time of her death that she was really his mother. Yet,
the conservatives dismissed this explanation as a poor excuse
and refused to be satisfied.[42]

The sweeping nature of the reform greatly increased the
intensity of factional strife. Factionalism was no longer a
matter of choice but a fact by force of circumstances. Wang
at first tried to persuade the elder statesmen to remain, but to
no avail.[43] Then the growing criticism of his reform became
unbearable to him. He became easily angered and sometimes
suffered from dizziness.[44] The reading of a critical memorial
made his hands tremble.[45] In retaliation he caused the dismissal of more than twenty censors.[46] He was especially determined to remove from the central government those who
opposed the hired-service system.[47] Believing so strongly in
the correctness of his own policies, Wang denounced all his
critics as worthless, ill-informed, convention-bound, or trouble-
making. He wanted the Emperor to listen to no one who
criticized the reform.[48] In this he was not entirely successful.
Wen Yen-po (1006–1097) remained as administrator of the
Bureau of Military Affairs for many years and often took a
stand against Wang.[49] Feng Ching (1021–1094) who also
differed with Wang, survived at the court longer than Wang
himself.[50] In the end Wang's insistence on his policies and
intolerance of even occasional criticism hurt him. Han Chiang,
who had associated with him at the beginning of the reform,
and Wu Ch'ung, his relative and another ranking minister,
both eventually disagreed with and left him. None of his
subordinates, especially after the dismissal of Tseng Pu, dared
to contradict him.[51]

The partisan attitude of the conservatives, when they took

over, was even more pronounced. Most of the New Policies were either abolished or radically revised, with no regard for their merits or for the consequences of restoring many old measures. The spirit in which this was done was vengeful. Wang's books were brushed aside in disgrace as if Wang had never been a leading scholar.[52] The conservatives lost little time in dismissing those who had supported the New Policies and replacing them with their own followers; and favoritism was actually more widespread than it had been among the reformers. For example, those in charge of the prefectural schools were appointed merely upon the recommendation of high officials, without first being given a test to ascertain their ability, as had previously been the case.[53] Ssu-ma Kuang, the leader of the antireformers, frankly stated that "unscrupulous officials were less desirable than stupid ones."[54] This was in sharp contrast to Wang's dictum cited above. In other words, the antireformers regarded all the reformers as unscrupulous and cared nothing about the administrative ability of their replacements, so long as the office routines were carried out in the old conventional manner. However worthy the antireform leaders were, their administration was not particularly successful. Nor was their attitude justifiable by the Confucian standard.

It was the antireform leaders who pushed factional strife to such a point that it never healed. It was they who put the existence of factions on an official basis by publishing at the court a list naming thirty officials as the members of the reform faction. Eighteen were listed under the leadership of Wang, who had already died, and twelve under the leadership of Ts'ai Ch'üeh. Although Ts'ai had no leading role during the reform phase until some time after Wang's retirement, he was greatly disliked by the antireformers, against whom he had deliberately instigated many charges.[55] This injection of personal revenge into factional strife had devastating consequences. It was soon reciprocated during the subsequent postreform; and the antireform leaders were destined to suffer even more punishment than they had administered to others.[56]

This disease of factionalism did not stop there. The antireform leaders also caused the dismissal of the southwestern moderates led by Su Shih and even such well-known conservatives as Fan Ch'un-jen, for no other reason than that these scholar-officials criticized the antireform for having gone to the other extreme.[57] In the end factional strife caught the antireform faction itself. It split into several cliques which attacked one another in the same manner, mostly for the sake of gaining personal power. This was a degeneration of political behavior to a level far below Confucian standards.

The postreform leaders counterattacked initially by compiling a denunciatory list of thirty names. Later Ts'ai Ching expanded the list indiscriminately to include two hundred and nine people, some of whom could not justly be classified as antireformers at all. Worse still, the list appeared in the form of stone tablets all over the country. This political persecution was accompanied by suppression of opinion. In all this Ts'ai's aim was neither to help the cause of reform, nor simply to heap revenge upon revenge, but to consolidate his own power.[58]

In retrospect, the political behavior of the bureaucrats had gone from bad to worse, farther and farther from the Confucian standards. In addition to the old faults of corruption and political maneuvering, favoritism had been intensified. However, Wang alone was not to blame. His opponents, in refusing to cooperate with him, in attacking those who did, and in practicing favoritism, were more responsible than he. Favoritism soon grew into factionalism, and factionalism degenerated from the level of policy disagreement to the level of revengeful persecution. The bureaucracy, instead of being reformed as Wang had hoped, now suffered from so many evils that inevitably only those who, like Ts'ai Ching, intrigued without regard for the Confucian standards managed to stay in power for a long period. The degeneration of the bureaucracy was soon followed by the collapse of the empire.

WANG AND THE VARIOUS TYPES OF BUREAUCRATS

The foregoing analysis of bureaucratic deviations gives only a partial explanation of the rise and fall of the New Policies. We need to know exactly which types of bureaucrats were in favor of the New Policies, which types were against them, and how these respective types degenerated in the course of the prolonged controversy, in order to understand more fully why the reform phase did not achieve a sustained success and why the postreform phase fared even worse.

Whether it is possible to classify the bureaucrats into political types as a historical interpretation of this era is an old question, to which historians have so far reacted in three ways, none of them satisfactory.

First, the traditional histories alleged that Wang surrounded himself with unscrupulous bureaucrats who were *hsiao-jen* (unworthy persons). The New Policies failed precisely because the morally upright *chün-tzu* (virtuous men) were on the conservative side. The use of this Confucian moralistic dichotomy of *chün-tzu* and *hsiao-jen* as a historical interpretation simply cannot explain why the conservatives also failed to produce a good administration.

Second, the works on Wang by the scholars Ts'ai, and later Liang, K'e, and Williamson, have demolished this allegation by showing that many bureaucrats who supported the New

Policies were by no means as bad as the traditional histories have unjustly pictured them to be. The refutations made by these scholars are based on the same criterion of Confucian morality as was the allegation. They merely underscore the difficulty of classifying the bureaucrats and confirm the fact that the measuring rod of Confucian morality has been found inapplicable.

Third, the recent scholars have classified the bureaucrats according to intellectual and socio-economic criteria. Their admirable research on the whole tends to leave an impression that, so far as their political behavior is concerned, there were not significant differences among the bureaucrats. The possibility of classifying them into political types is thus dismissed. But can we really agree that while there are different kinds of individuals in the bureaucracy, they as a group constitute a single type and that their political behavior is more or less the same?

What we shall attempt here constitutes a new approach. Without minimizing the manifold difficulties and pitfalls in this attempt, several qualifications should be made from the very outset. First, political beings, especially those whose circumstances were complicated and who were of a period when few reliable records were kept, can never be wholly reduced to simple types. Types only serve to highlight a few noteworthy traits. Second, these types and traits should be based upon behavioral factors and not upon moral judgments, though the socially justified and unjustified behavior patterns are objectively distinguishable without great difficulty. Third, a type does not represent a fixed position in a mechanical scale. It actually indicates a range of behavioral patterns which overlap. Fourth, it follows that in classifying particular individuals there are bound to be borderline cases. Fifth, it must be remembered that the bureaucrats after all had much in common. The traits, while far more characteristic of one type than of another, are to be distinguished in the relative rather than in the exclusive sense.

I have surveyed the biographical data on several dozens of officials in this period, though I am concentrating here upon only a few of Wang's close associates.[59] The approach, in essence, is to reëxamine the historical data in order to arrive at some classification that is sociologically tenable. This approach has previously been used in a test case of the various bureaucrats connected with the reform led by Fan Chung-yen.[60] What is intended here is another test case. It is hoped that this approach, with due adaptation, may become applicable to the Sung period as a whole and even to other periods in Chinese history.

The classification used here identifies among the officials three general types: the idealistic scholar-official, the career-minded bureaucrat, and the abusive bureaucrat. Within each general type there are specific types. The idealistic scholar-officials have four traits: personal integrity, recognized scholarship, a devotion to high ideals, and a firm belief in their political principles, which they put before personal advantage. They are roughly identifiable with, though not exactly identical with, the *chün-tzu*, well known in traditional historiography. Their common creed was best expressed by the pioneer reformer Fan Chung-yen: "to take the world as one's own responsibility." This does not mean that they were faultless. A certain degree of tolerance must be allowed for their failure to follow their own ideals. This general type in Wang's time was further divided into three specific types or groups: the northern conservatives, the southwestern moderates, and the southern reformers.

The career-minded bureaucrats were the kind normally found in practically all governments, who realistically placed their career interests before other values. In comparison with the idealistic type, their scholarship was far less profound, their devotion to high ideals was much less noticeable, if indeed it existed at all, and their political principles were more or less subordinated to political expediency. However, in personal integrity they met the average standard of conduct determined by social convention, and they were accordingly clearly distinguishable from the abusive type. Despite such poor practices as indulgence in certain mild forms of corruption, the defects in their personal behavior were on the whole not very serious. The common sentiment of this type was best expressed by Wen Yen-po in two statements, the first of which is famous: "Your Majesty rules the empire with the bureaucrats, not with the people." [61] His second statement, though not well known, succinctly defines bureaucratic careerism: "Who does not like high positions and honors? But one should also think of the state." [62] In Wang's time this careerist type was further divisible into two specific types: the conformist and the executive.

The conformists were no doubt the overwhelming majority in the bureaucracy. Their career interests were best protected under the existing system and its mode of operation. Generally speaking, they took little initiative in making policy changes and tended to object to drastic innovations. They supported the conservatives against Wang's reform; but when the reform had become the established order, they conformed with it. The conformist type is roughly identifiable with what the traditional historiography has described as "scrupulous officials" or "principled officials" (hsün-li) and "good officials" (liang-li), though these two traditional designations generally refer to the territorial officials rather than those serving at the court.

The executive type, on the other hand, was energetic, ambitious, and aggressive, with superior talent in addition to administrative ability. These men had initiative, supported radical policy changes, and carried out new policies effectively, sometimes because they provided an opportunity for rapid career advancement and sometimes because they were in accord with their own political beliefs or inclinations. Many of Wang's close associates belonged to this type. There is not even a rough equivalent of this type in traditional historiography. It may be said to be a composite of what have been known as "able officials" (neng-li), "capable officials" (kan-ts'ai), "officials good at administration" (shan li-shih or ch'ang yü li-shih), and other similar descriptions.

The abusive bureaucrats were the unprincipled and unscrupulous ones, intensely interested in their official position, not as a career but as a means to an end, so that they might use their power and influence to increase their selfish materialistic gain. Their value orientation is to be found in the previously cited dictum of Teng Chien, "Despise and curse me as much as you like, but I am going to enjoy this good office." In Wang's time the abusive bureaucrats divided into two specific types: the corrupt and the manipulative. The corrupt type used what power they had by virtue of their offices to enrich themselves. They reacted unfavorably to the reform, which attempted to improve the government administration and to eliminate embezzlement and other corrupt practices. But they did not object to the postreform, when maladministration started at the very top of the government. The traditional historiography has described them as "corrupt officials" (t'an-kuan or wu-li).

The manipulative type was more than corrupt. Energetic and aggressive, like the executive type, they directed their efforts through irregular tactics and unprincipled maneuvers, first to the enhancement of their power beyond what was normally inherent in their office, and then to indulgence in corruption, often on a large scale. They ostensibly followed the reform policy, because the reform measures gave more power to the offices that dealt with financial matters. During the postreform they became as prominent, or notorious, as they were powerful. In traditional terms, they have been described not only as corrupt but also as "power-manipulating" (*nung-ch'üan*), "power-usurping" (*shan-ch'üan*), and the like.

The classification is thus complete, with all types defined. Most of these types are readily understandable, but two — the career-minded executive and the abusive manipulative type — require further clarification by comparison and concrete illustration. Individual cases among Wang's associates serve this purpose very well. Four have been chosen here: Tseng Pu, Lü Hui-ch'ing, Chang Ch'un, and Ts'ai Ch'üeh; the last is not to be confused with Ts'ai Ching of postreform notoriety. Specific behavioral traits have been taken from biographical data [63] and are listed in Table 1.

Table 1. Traits of bureaucrats of the executive type, as seen in Wang's associates.

	Tseng	Lü	Chang	Ts'ai
Characteristic				
Superior administrative ability	X	X	X	X
Aggressiveness, especially in political tactics	X	X	X	X
Superior skill in preparing documents	X	X	X	?
Eloquence, especially in debate	X	?	X	?
Considerable scholarship	X	X	o	o
Deviational *				
Ingratiation with superiors	?	X	X	X
Betrayal of associates and friends	?	X	?	?
Formation of a personal clique	o	o	X	X
Friendly relations with eunuchs	o	o	X	o
Deliberate persecution of opponents	o	X	X	X
Personal or family financial corruption	o	X	X	X

* to a certain extent akin to the characteristic traits of the manipulative type

It is evident from this table that Tseng is the best repre-
sentative of the executive type, Lü next to him, while Chang
and Ts'ai may be classified as borderline cases between the
executive type and the manipulative type. A brief review
of the evidence substantiates this analysis. Tseng was a
family friend of Wang and in his younger days his political ideas were greatly influenced by Wang.[64] In the preparation of laws and regulations for the reform measures,
Tseng played a more important part than Lü, contrary to the
impression given in history.[65] For several years Wang relied
more heavily upon Tseng than upon Lü, though Lü was also
important. Yet the Emperor did not like Tseng as well as Lü.[66]
Furthermore, Tseng lost favor with Wang when he proved
that Wang had an incorrect idea as to the execution of the
State Trade System. Lü, on the other hand, maneuvered with
sufficient skill to become Wang's successor and ousted Tseng
from the court.[67] Tseng returned to power during the early
part of the postreform phase, when he was the only reform
leader to advocate a policy of reconciliation toward those who
had opposed the reform, in the interest of national unity. The
philosopher Chu Hsi, in condemning Wang's followers in
general, regarded Tseng as a commendable exception.[68] The
Sung dynastic history has failed to take note of this exception
and has dogmatically done Tseng an injustice by including him
with Wang's other associates in "biographies of wicked min-
isters" (Chien-ch'en-chuan).[69]

By comparison, Chang Ch'un and Ts'ai Ch'üeh appear in
a much worse light.[70] They contributed little in initiating and
introducing the reform measures, but they gained power later,
especially after Wang's retirement. During the postreform
phase they deliberately persecuted their conservative opponents, and Chang Ch'un even conspired with eunuchs in
palace intrigues. Nor can Lü, Chang, and Ts'ai compare

favorably with Tseng in personal integrity. Lü allegedly allowed relatives to extort money from the wealthy people; Chang's father forcibly occupied properties belonging to other people; and Ts'ai sent his brother to use office funds for private profit. Ironically, Tseng was driven from power by Ts'ai Ching, who conspired to obtain fabricated confessions from Tseng's sons by torture, in the hope of implicating Tseng on a false charge of corruption.

It would be a mistake, however, to praise any bureaucrat of the executive type unduly. Tseng and all the others had a tendency to gather more and more power into their own hands. This tendency might lead to the deviational traits which, when they became pronounced and dominant, were precisely the characteristics of the manipulative type. Chang, a borderline case, and Ts'ai Ch'üeh, probably the same, may be regarded as forerunners of Ts'ai Ching, a manipulative official. From this viewpoint there is an evolutionary relation, first between Wang's preference for administrative ability and the executive type, and secondly between the deviations of the executive type and the rise of the manipulative type. This is the main basis for the conservatives' moral indignation against all the reformers.

This classification of the bureaucrats into distinctive types is not a static one convenient merely to distinguish them. When the historical context is introduced, this classification immediately gives a dynamic picture of the evolution of the political situation. When the New Policies were first introduced by Wang and his executive-type associates during the reform phase, they encountered so much difficulty because the conformist type, the majority in the bureaucracy, opposed them with all its power. But when the New Policies were later revived by the manipulative type during the postreform phase they met with little obstruction, because by this time the manipulative type commanded enough power to compel the conformist type to obey; also, the New Policies were in fact no longer so new as to make conformance difficult. However, abuse from above and mere conformity within the bureaucracy, without the original exuberant energy of the reform and without Wang's degree of bureaucratic idealism, could only contribute to a dismal end.

This analysis of the relation between the various types of bureaucrats and the evolution of the political situation may be graphically presented. The diagram lists both general and specific types of bureaucrats. The vertical line indicates the split between the reformers and their opponents when Wang was in power; the area below the dotted line indicates the area of power consolidation that Ts'ai Ching was able to dominate during the postreform phase.

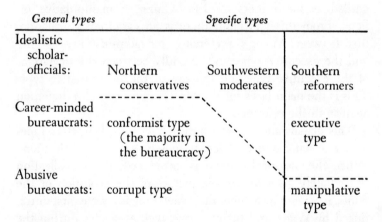

General types	Specific types		
Idealistic scholar-officials:	Northern conservatives	Southwestern moderates	Southern reformers
Career-minded bureaucrats:	conformist type (the majority in the bureaucracy)		executive type
Abusive bureaucrats:	corrupt type		manipulative type

Wang's group was a minority even among the idealistic scholar-officials. Nor were the executive bureaucrats numerous. To the best of his judgment Wang refused to put the manipulative type into power. On the other hand, the majority in the bureaucracy were against him: the conservative and the moderate idealistic scholar-officials in principle, the conformists by virtue of their dislike of radical change, and the corrupt because of the disadvantages to their own interests. Wang had to rely principally upon the support of the Emperor.

The situation was vastly different under Ts'ai. By this time many venerated scholar-officials had died, and those who survived were banished by Ts'ai. Absolutism had grown considerably and Ts'ai turned it to his own advantage. The executive bureaucrats, after regaining power in the early part of the postreform, were once again removed either through their own mutual antagonisms or by the maneuvers of Ts'ai. Meanwhile, the conformists had become accustomed to the reform measures, which were no longer novelties; they were also fearful of the political persecution under Ts'ai. Since Ts'ai himself was corrupt, the bureaucrats of the corrupt type gladly followed suit. Thus the reform gradually degenerated into maladministration.

This classification is no more than a test of a new approach. It serves the purpose of clarifying the political behavior of many officials at the time, the varying attitudes of these officials toward the reform and its aftermath, and the eventual failure of the New Policies. On the other hand, as it now stands, this classification is schematic. We need many more analytic studies of political behavior, particularly in individual biographies. Only then will it be possible to determine more accurately how a particular individual may or may not fit into a definite type, with certain necessary qualifications and modifications. Only then will it be possible to understand more fully how a historical trend — political degeneration in this case — manifests itself in the actual career of the individuals.

V

The New Policies and
Government Operations

THE CLERICAL SUBBUREAUCRACY

The clerical subbureaucracy is of particular interest because
it is often overlooked, although obviously the actual government operations, insofar as they reached the people, were
carried on through the clerks. The importance of the clerks
became more evident during the Sung period than before.
Administrative procedure, especially in fiscal and legal matters, became more detailed and complicated; furthermore,
printing made feasible the extensive use of forms and documents. As a result, the clerks who took charge of an increasing
amount of routine became a considerably specialized body.
As there existed no formal training in such skills and little in
the way of a formal recruitment program for such personnel,
the positions were filled largely by the descendants, relatives,
and family friends of the existing personnel. Many clerks in
the central government tended to become permanent residents
in and around the capital. Most of the clerks in the local
government were natives of the area. In this sense, the clerks
may be regarded as a local subbureaucracy at the lowest echelon
of the administration. By law and custom their social status
was greatly inferior to that of the officials in the civil service
who formed the national bureaucracy;[1] but this does not mean
that the clerks were functionally unimportant so far as government operation was concerned.

Wang, zealously concerned with the reform of the official bureaucracy, could not possibly ignore the need for a related improvement in the clerical subbureaucracy. Furthermore, the New Policies, in enlarging the scope and number of government operations, inevitably placed in the hands of the clerks a greater share of responsibility than ever before. Consequently, the clerical subbureaucracy inevitably helped to condition the outcome of the New Policies.

Though an estimate is difficult, one can readily infer the large size of the clerical staff in the central government from the fact that during the New Policy era the Finance Commission alone occupied more than 1,080 compartments of rooms filled with files.[2] The research of Miyazaki reveals that these clerks in the central government drew small salaries that were hardly adequate incomes. The clerks in the local government offices, before the New Policies were put into effect, had no regular salaries at all; instead, they received some compensation for their services from the miscellaneous tax revenues.[3]

While the officials were subject to transfer from one place to another, the clerks stayed on in a particular government office rather permanently. It has been said that, although the officials were not "feudalistic" (*feng-chien*), the clerks were, in the sense that they had a *de facto* tenure of a local or territorial nature. With their long-standing and intimate knowledge of local office matters, the clerks were often able to influence the administrative decisions of the officials, who were less familiar with them.[4] These clerks had no hope of advancement and few of them had moral scruples. Their chief concern, as Wang pointed out, was to carry on corrupt practices by deceiving the officials.[5] The clerks handled many financial matters without being subject to close supervision; also, many people came to tempt them with bribes.[6] It was no secret that they conspired with merchants and connived with corrupt officials.[7]

As Miyazaki indicates, Wang was keenly aware of the need for reform in this subbureaucracy. First, he reduced the number of the clerks in government service. Second, he increased the pay for those in the central government who had been drawing regular salaries and put the previously unsalaried clerks in the local government on a salary basis. Third, he was in favor of promoting meritorious clerks, after due examination, to the rank of civil servants in officialdom. Fourth, he demanded that the clerks be subject to effective supervision and to heavy penalties for corruption.[8] This significant reform was called the Granary System (*Ts'ang fa*). Granary here is a general term which refers to both the granaries where the revenue grains were stored and the local government treasuries. Many clerical duties, and also many corrupt practices, were connected with these sources. Moreover, the clerks were to receive their salaries from these same sources.[9] Wang's ultimate ideal, in line with his faith in the ancient institutional pattern described by the *Chou-li*, was to merge the clerks and the officials into one class and ultimately to integrate them, as well as the farmers and the soldiers, all into a single class.[10] In upholding such an ideal Wang overlooked the fact that class structure had already become rigid, social groups well differentiated, and vocations increasingly specialized; there could never be only one class.[11]

Apart from this egalitarian but impractical ideal, Wang's Granary System worked with impressive results. He argued that it was better to pay the clerks according to government regulations than to overlook or, in effect, permit them to take money in violation of the law.[12] The resulting increase in the government budget was after all not a very heavy burden. It was adequately met by the effective financing of the reform measures, under which the local government took upon itself to manage such miscellaneous revenues as those from markets (*ch'ang*), factories (*fang*, particularly of wine and liquor), and ferries (*chin-tu*). Heretofore these had been assigned or "farmed out" to the clerks as compensation for their services. According to Wang, the local government administration was thus put on a sound and reasonable basis without having to increase the tax burden upon the people.[13] At the same time, the required vigilant supervision of the clerks and the heavy penalties imposed on them for corruption did improve the standard of local government considerably. Even Wang's opponents admitted this.[14]

But the clerical subbureaucracy was by no means so easily cured of its evils. The salary they now received could not possibly equal one-half of the income they had previously managed to secure through corruption.[15] Nor was the new supervision adequate to catch them all. Many of the New Policies aroused complaint and failed to realize their objectives largely because the clerks who helped to administer them found in them means of embezzlement and extortion. There are numerous examples. Whether the state farming loans helped those who needed them or were forced upon those who would not be benefited by them at all depended in large part upon whether the clerks abided by the spirit of the system, which was often not the case.[16] The number of the ever-normal granaries (*ch'ang-p'ing-ts'ang*) increased under the reform to about 500 throughout the nation; they were established to aid government financing and for use when necessary to equalize distribution. But through poor administration they helped the corrupt officials and clerks more than they ever helped the people.[17] The Land Survey and Equitable Tax System was an important reform to eliminate tax evasion and unfair burdens. However, the actual

surveying, recording, and reporting passed through the hands
of the clerks, who easily connived with dishonest officials and
wealthy families to defeat the law. The whole system degenerated into a farce during the postreform phase.[18] The services for the local government were put on the basis of a commuted tax under the reform; they were returned to rotating
assignment during the antireform; and the commutation
method was restored during the postreform. Both tax assessment and rotating assignment involved the clerks, who helped
to determine the extent of a family's property and also its
tax burden. During the abrupt changes back and forth, many
records were deliberately hidden by the clerks or reportedly
lost. This created abundant opportunity for abuse.[19] An equally
unhappy example was the State Trade System. The large
merchants were deprived of many advantages when the government dealt directly with the smaller merchants at officially
regulated prices. Yet the smaller merchants, to whom the law
extended loan facilities, did not really profit much. Nor did
the results necessarily benefit the consumers. Actually, considerable profit went to the clerks and, through them, to the
abusive bureaucrats.[20]

It is no exaggeration, therefore, to contend that Wang's
reform measures were defeated in part by the combination of
abusive bureaucrats and the incorrigible subbureaucracy. In
this sense there is a good deal of truth in a major criticism
of the New Policies that was made by Wang's opponents,
namely, that these measures inadvertently or necessarily put
more administrative power into the hands of the undesirable
elements and thus created even greater opportunities for abuse
and manipulation. On the other hand, Wang's opponents
were themselves unable to offer any constructive proposals
as to how the evils of the subbureaucracy might be cured.
The local government administration deteriorated progres-

sively through the antireform and the postreform.[21] By the time of the Southern Sung most services for the local government, in accordance with the New Policies, were rendered by hired personnel. In other words, there were now more clerks than ever, and the government suffered from an increased dependence upon this greatly expanded subbureaucracy. This same situation lasted through the Ch'ing period to recent times.[22]

CENTRALIZATION AND CONFORMITY

One important characteristic of the Sung government operation was the trend toward increasing centralization. This trend had actually become noticeable before the Sung during the chaotic period of the Five Dynasties, when it was a direct reaction to local military power and usurpation. At the very beginning of the Sung, centralization was already pronounced. A distinction must be made, however, between centralization for the security of the state and the centralization of financial administration.[23] The Sung empire from the outset took measures to prevent the danger of regional usurpation by keeping its best army under the direct command of the central government, by instituting a close watch over all local military officers, and by giving the civilian territorial officials a larger measure of power than they had ever possessed under the previous regimes. Under these circumstances, the financial administration of the local government was placed largely in the hands of these civilian officials, subject to only general requirements imposed by the central government.

The centralization of financial administration became established only with the coming of the New Policies, which, in administering an expanding state finance, instituted various fiscal controls. For example, the central government began to direct the local government units to collect tax revenues according to the estimations made by the central government; the tax quotas were no longer based, as before, upon the varying reports of the local government units, nor upon their pleas or excuses for a lesser amount.[24]

This financial centralization led to a similar trend in personnel policy. The Sung empire treated its high-ranking officials with unusual courtesy and consideration. When they lost favor at the court, they were often given respectable posts in local government. When the New Policies were first introduced, many elder statesmen, and other lesser officials in the local government, flatly refused to obey the central government's directives to carry out those New Policies to which they took strong exception. Wang could tolerate no such obstruction. He gradually removed these opponents from office and replaced them with officials who obeyed orders. He thus, in effect, curtailed the courtesy formerly due to the high-ranking officials, introduced more centralized control over appointments, and achieved what he believed to be the necessary degree of bureaucratic conformity. He was able to bring about these changes because the absolute power of the emperor was then on his side.

Another aspect of further centralization was the concentration of power in the executive branch at the very top of the government organization. Before the reform, as E. A. Kracke's standard work on the Sung civil service shows, a clear division of jurisdiction existed between the Secretariat-chancellery (Chung-shu Men-hsia), which was the executive branch in charge of general administration, the Bureau of Military Affairs (Shu-mi-yüan), and the Finance Commission (San-ssu).[25] Wang was unable to remove Wen Yen-po from the

Bureau of Military Affairs, but he undermined some of Wen's power by intervening in the appointments of military personnel.[26] In addition, he superimposed a unified control over the Finance Commission by setting up the Finance Planning Commission to study and recommend financial reforms.[27] Owing to the persistent objection that this new commission was out of place in the government structure, it was later absorbed into the Secretariat-chancellery.[28] The fact remained that the executive department no longer observed the former division of jurisdiction; it now had direct control over the Finance Commission, and without its approval no regulations pertaining to state finance could be put into effect.[29]

A similar change took place within the Finance Commission. Previously its jurisdiction had been divided among three offices, hence its name, San-ssu or "three offices": the Census Office (Hu-pu), in charge of the revenues based upon the classification of households; the Funds or Fiscal Office (Tu-chih), in charge of appropriations and expenditures, and the Office of Salt and Iron (Yen T'ieh), in charge of these and similar state monopolies.[30] Considerable confusion was created at the beginning of the reform when the Court of Agricultural Supervision (Ssu-nung-shih), whose main responsibility had originally been the ever-normal granaries (Ch'ang-p'ing-ts'ang), was given the task of using the granary resources to finance many important reform measures.[31] And for a brief period during the progress of the reform two new offices were set up: the Financial Examination Office (Chang-ssu) and the Auditing Office (K'uai-chi-ssu).[32] In the end, after prolonged friction, the Finance Commission was allowed to reunite all these functions, but only under the guidance of the executive.[33] The accepted practice now was for the privy councilors in charge of the executive (better known by their informal title of tsai-hsiang) to be in direct control of the reserve funds, in order to implement the policies recommended by them.[34]

Wang left a legacy of strong executive power. Despite their numerous criticisms, the antireformers made no effort to reverse this legacy when they themselves came into power.[35] This powerful centralization became a permanent feature of the government structure.[36]

The Sung government operation was also characterized by efforts to enforce conformity. Conformity among the bureaucrats was not the rule when Wang initiated his reform. On the contrary, as we have seen, the period was noted for its robust and creative Confucianism and its many new and diverse opinions. However, Wang was so devoted to his own unconventional ideas that he became increasingly doctrinaire and intolerant of other ideas, which he often dismissed as merely conventional, worthless, and obstructive. On one occasion he complained to the Emperor, "If anyone at the court is permitted to obstruct policies with different ideas, how can the principles of good government ever be realized? In my humble opinion, unless the entrusted officials at the court have the same purpose, the same beliefs, and cooperate in unity, nothing can really be accomplished at all." [37] In other words, Wang believed that conformity was required for efficient government operation. In reforming the National Academy and the examination system, his intention was to produce and to recruit like-minded bureaucrats. The Emperor agreed with Wang on the desirability of unifying Confucianism by preparing and officially proclaiming the authoritative interpretations of the classics.[38] This not only infuriated the conservative scholars, but also failed to achieve its real objective. The Emperor soon discovered that the result was not unity, but conformity. He commented: "The court wants to reform the candidates through the interpretations of the classics. Eight or nine out of ten candidates have changed accordingly. Yet they have merely stolen what others said without really trying to gain a real understanding." [39] This was not at all surprising, for the candidates at the examinations parroted the writings of Wang and his son in a number of essays which they prepared beforehand. [40]

The antireformers, equally if not even more dogmatically, countered by removing from the bureaucracy those who supported the reform. Not knowing what to do with the students at the National Academy, who were greatly influenced by Wang's ideas, they simply ordered the Academy to admit no more students. [41] Meanwhile they hoped that with the appointment of their own followers in the prefectural schools the intellectual atmosphere and political opinion among the students would gradually turn in their favor.

Bureaucratic conformity reached an unprecedented height under Ts'ai Ching's postreform. The books written by the antireformers were banned. The prefectural schools, upon orders, provided "self-indicting study rooms" (tzu-sung chai). While no detail of this measure has been recorded, its aim was to have those students who had openly declared themselves in favor of the antireform assigned to such rooms; there they were to do further reading and thinking in order to correct their allegedly mistaken opinions. The imposed conformity reached a point where thousands of examination papers all read alike. Candidates learned, from political persecution, not even to express such commonplace ideas as "demobilization so that the people may rest, preservation of resources by economy, elimination of nonessential public works, and of corruption in bureaucratic recruitment," for these were looked upon as implied criticisms of the administration. [42] Another factor which contributed to conformity in the bureaucracy was the growing activity of the Palace Guard Commission (Huang-ch'eng-ssu), which was in charge of intelligence work in the capital. Saeki has shown that this commission resorted to the employment of *agents provocateurs* and by this and other means trapped people into voicing criticisms; it also made false reports to incriminate the innocent.[43]

The paralyzing and suffocating conformity, an almost unbelievable change from the creative Confucianism of the preceding era, had no single cause. Increased conformity was to a certain extent inevitable under a growing centralization; but it far exceeded normal limits when the tremendous power created through centralization was abused by a bureaucrat like Ts'ai Ching. Wang probably had never realized that his New Policies, by strengthening centralization and requiring what he believed to be necessary conformity, would lead to such unhappy results.

ABSOLUTISM

The operation of the Sung government was also deeply affected by the trend toward absolutism. Absolutism had two essential features: the final power of the emperor, and, closely connected with it, palace politics and intrigues. This final power was not normally despotic, inasmuch as it was circumscribed by the conventional Confucian sanctions, by customary bounds, and also by the fact that power was shared in varying degrees with the bureaucrats. The sharing of power was especially notable in the Northern Sung period, when the emperors often deferred to the opinions of high-ranking officials. These officials regarded themselves as the apostles of Confucianism, with ideological authority. Furthermore, as the political leaders among the bureaucrats, they did exercise considerable power in the form of articulate political opinion and in the form of political pressure. But, however much power these officials enjoyed, it was only a derivative power, delegated by the sovereign and remaining always within a limit imposed upon it by absolutism. In times of stress absolutism tended to grow and correspondingly to reduce the power of the bureaucrats by lowering this limit.

To introduce his sweeping reforms and to overcome strong opposition within the bureaucracy, Wang had to rely mainly upon the support of the Emperor. Fortunately, the Emperor respected Wang as a teacher, told him to dispense with formalities, asked for his frank opinions, and accepted them.[44] For a long time "the Emperor and Wang seemed to be one person," for the Emperor was persuaded by Wang to keep no secrets from him.[45] Moreover, in his enthusiasm for the reform, Wang advised the Emperor to be "firm and strong," in the hope of silencing the opposition.[46] The resulting high pressure from the court was effective. For example, Ssu-ma Kuang, for several years after his dismissal from the court at the beginning of the reform, refrained from open criticism of the prevailing policies.[47] To this extent Wang furthered the growth of absolutism.

No emperor's confidence in any bureaucrat has been limitless or lasting, however. Absolutism carries with it the fear that an official might become too powerful. The example of repeated usurpations during the Five Dynasties which preceded the Sung empire helped to keep this fear alive.[48] The reform of Fan Chung-yen, for example, was put to an abrupt end when his opponents warned the Emperor that some of Fan's associates were engaging in an alleged conspiracy to commit high treason, with possible help from the Liao empire.[49] Fear of any potential, or even imaginary, threat to the throne has always prevented emperors from placing too much confidence in any particular official. All the previous works on Wang

have generally held that, at least at the beginning of the New
Policy era, Wang did enjoy the complete trust of the Emperor. This is subject to two qualifications, however. First,
although the Emperor did not seriously doubt Wang's loyalty,
he was probably afraid that by giving Wang too much power
he might arouse the disloyalty of other leading officials. When
the New Policies were first introduced, rumors began to spread
that in the midst of the popular discontent Han Ch'i, the most
venerated elder statesman of the time, might force their abolition by an armed intervention.[50] The aim of these rumors was
doubtless to arouse the fear of the Emperor in order to defeat
the New Policies, as similar rumors had successfully ousted
Fan Chung-yen, and they probably did prevent him from
supporting them fully. Secondly, there is strong evidence to
suggest that the Emperor's confidence in Wang himself was
less than complete. For many years during the New Policy
era he retained Wen Yen-po, Wang's firm opponent, as head
of the Bureau of Military Affairs, and ignored Wang's complaints against him.

The Emperor's great faith in Wang finally weakened when
Empress Dowager Hsüan-jen and others in the palace warned
him that the rampant discontent caused by the State Trade
System and the Guild Exemption Tax might lead to a disturbance in the capital.[51] His doubts increased when inquiries
conducted by Tseng Pu revealed, contrary to Wang's assur-
ances, that there were indeed many justifiable complaints.
Wang was hurt and soon thereafter asked to be relieved. After
permitting Wang to leave the court for the governorship in
Nanking, the Emperor for the first time issued a special edict
ordering frank criticism of the reform in order to rectify mis-
takes, and certain reform measures were temporarily sus-
pended.[52] He soon recalled Wang for another period of service, but although he continued to believe in the essential

soundness of the reform and kept it in operation throughout his lifetime, even after Wang's final retirement, his enthusiasm had noticeably declined. At the time of Wang's first resignation from the court the Emperor stated: "After all, we should carefully abide by those old institutions that are good. It is unreasonable to change all of them without giving due consideration to the consequences." [53] He thus withdrew his wholehearted support from the reform because of an uneasiness stemming basically from a deep fear of any possible impingement upon the security of the regime. This lack of full imperial support was a heavy, if not decisive, blow to the effectiveness of the reform.

The parasite nurtured by absolutism was palace politics. The weakening of the Emperor's confidence in Wang affected the palace personnel. Wang succeeded in persuading him to silence the opposition in the bureaucracy but never the eunuchs, the Empress Dowager, other palace ladies, and their relatives. The friction that existed between Wang and the eunuchs has generally not been noticed by the historians. While the Sung eunuchs did not have much power, they still had some influence upon the Emperor.[54] Wang told the Emperor on several occasions that the government's policies could be defeated by the bad influence of eunuchs.[55] The Emperor replied, however, that he rather liked their "smooth" service.[56] Wang then advised him not to believe the unreliable reports of the Palace Guard Commission,[57] but the Emperor seems not to have accepted this advise. Meanwhile the State Trade System and the Guild Exemption Tax, which eliminated official contact between the merchants and the eunuchs, caused the latter to lose bribes and other opportunities for corruption.[58] Both the eunuchs of the Palace Guard Commission and those working in the palace sought to compensate their losses by asking for higher pay, citing the increase in the clerks' wages as a precedent. The Emperor favored compensating them from the state trade and tax surplus, which seemed reasonable; but Wang's objections deterred him.[59]

The eunuchs made their resentment against Wang quite obvious. The eunuchs at the Directorate of Astronomical Observation (Ssu-t'ien-chien) had earlier interpreted certain omens as indicating the desirability of dismissing Wang and replacing him with someone from the northern areas.[60] They now tried to embarrass Wang by requiring him, contrary to custom, to dismount outside the palace gate. Wang's horse was hurt in this incident.[61] Encouraging the eunuchs were Wang's two political opponents, Wen Yen-po and Feng Ching. Wen, whose duties at the Board of Military Affairs included supervision of the Palace Guard Commission, was friendly to the eunuchs and often gave them rapid promotion.[62] Feng also supported the eunuchs, particularly on the issue of their pay increase.[63]

The eunuchs found other allies among the relatives of the Empress who did not like Wang, for Wang had changed regulations so as to reduce the imperial favors to which they had been entitled. Some of these relatives also opposed the State Trade System and the Guild Exemption Tax, since these measures were either contrary to their financial interests or made their dealings with the merchants less profitable.[64] Still more important was the fact that the Empress Dowager Hsüan-jen, a native of the North, had disapproved of the reform from the beginning and had argued against it with the Emperor.[65]

A combination of all these factors led the people in the palace to warn the Emperor that the discontent caused by the State Trade System and the Guild Exemption Tax might lead to an uprising in the capital. Wang's position became untenable when some of the charges made by the palace people against the reform turned out to have some basis. At this crucial moment, the famine in the North compounded Wang's political misfortune. Cheng Hsia presented his "portrait of the refugees" that so shocked the Emperor. History has regarded this portrait as the main cause of Wang's first demotion. A closer examination of the HCP reveals that the portrait merely served as a precipitating factor after Wang's position had already been weakened by palace politics, especially by the influence of the eunuchs.[66]

Palace politics grew in both magnitude and intensity during the antireform and the postreform, another fact that history has generally underestimated. The reform came to an end with the death of Emperor Shen-tsung in 1085. Emperor Che-tsung, who succeeded him, was only ten years old, and his grandmother, Empress Dowager Hsüan-jen, acted as regent until her death in 1093. She pursued the antireform policy and put the conservatives into power, led briefly by Ssu-ma Kuang. Many of these conservatives were, like herself, from the northern area.[67]

During her regency a few eunuchs who were particularly loyal to the former emperor were dismissed. Her own favorite eunuchs were entrusted with her imperial seal and the power to handle state papers when she herself fell ill. These eunuchs also had cordial relations with several leading conservatives at the court, which indicates that the latter were not as idealistic as they claimed.[68]

The young Emperor was quite unhappy under these circumstances. He adored his late father, sympathized with the reform, and remembered that he had been put on the throne at the initial suggestion of Chang Ch'un, a reformer. He disliked the antireform leaders, who asked his grandmother to exert pressure upon him in the hope that he would pursue her policy in the future.[69] The choice of his consort, Empress Chao-tz'u, made by his domineering grandmother, added to his dissatisfaction.[70]

When the young Emperor himself came to the throne the postreform policy was immediately put into effect. The reformers were recalled to power, but their idealistic fervor was now greatly reduced. The New Policies were revived, but with neither improvement nor correction of errors. Chang Ch'un and a few other members of the reform faction formed a personal clique. Apparently very familiar with palace politics, they lost little time in telling the Emperor that the late Empress Dowager had intended to dethrone him. An investigation was ordered, to obtain confessions of this conspiracy from suspected eunuchs.[71] Ch'en Yen, the most powerful eunuch under the late Empress Dowager, was executed and others of her favorites were exiled.[72]

Empress Chao-tz'u was still in the way. It happened that the heirless Emperor was fond of a lady-in-waiting named Liu, who gave birth to a prince. Some eunuchs who were partial to this lady accused the Empress of resorting to black magic with evil intentions. These eunuchs joined forces with the reform clique in the court and, with the Emperor's permission, launched a secret palace investigation at which torture produced some false confessions in support of the accusation. Some thirty eunuchs and palace maids underwent torture and several had their tongues cut out. The Empress was thereupon banished to a nunnery and Lady Liu became the new empress, though her baby prince presently died.[73]

It was evident that Emperor Che-tsung had gone too far. When Hui-tsung, a younger brother, succeeded in 1100, he took the advice of Tseng Pu and pursued a reconciliatory policy toward the antireformers. In line with this policy, he restored the Empress Chao-tz'u to the palace; the rival Empress

Liu, unable to accept this reversal and humiliation, committed suicide.[74] Yet the reconciliatory policy of Tseng did not last long, for he was soon replaced by Ts'ai Ching, the manipulative bureaucrat. One reason for Ts'ai's success in gaining power was that he collaborated closely with the eunuch T'ung Kuan in courting the Emperor's favor with an excess of luxuries from the Yangtze delta region. By taking advantage of the Emperor's weakness for luxuries, both Ts'ai and T'ung retained their power for a long time. While Ts'ai practically monopolized the political power at the court, T'ung took over the military command of the army, which no Sung eunuch had ever done.

It thus becomes evident that palace politics were connected not only with Wang's fall from power but also with the abrupt changes of the antireform and of the postreform, and finally with the deterioration of the postreform.

VI

Service for Local Government: A Case Study

The rise and fall of the New Policies has been analyzed thus far in general terms, in the context of the political thought of the time, the political behavior of the bureaucrats, and several characteristics of Sung government operation. It has been shown that Wang's theories and actions went far beyond changes in laws and in government policies but actually aimed at bringing about institutional changes, especially in those political institutions that concerned the bureaucracy itself and in other institutions established by government initiative. However, since there has been no discussion of any particular segment of the New Policies, I now propose to support my general analysis by a case study.

I have chosen the reform of the local government service (*chih-i*, sometimes simply known as *i*, and the system as *i-fa*) for three reasons. First, this particular reform precipitated one of the most bitter controversies of the time. Previously the services for the local government had been requisitioned by rotating assignment. Under the reform, despite incessant objections, the services were rendered by hired personnel, who were paid out of taxes levied for this purpose. Secondly, the previous works on Wang and on this period have been almost invariably inaccurate with regard to the nature of this service. This should be remedied by introducing the research on this service by Nieh Ch'ung Ch'i and that by Sogabe Shizuo, as neither seems to be sufficiently known to many interested students. Thirdly, the reform of the local government service system has a significance which goes beyond its scope, for it was either directly or indirectly connected with several other reform measures, like the *pao-chia* policing system, the salaries for the clerks, and the land survey and equitable tax. From this viewpoint, it may well be regarded as central to the entire New Policies program and an excellent illustration for our purpose here.

THE SERVICE SYSTEM BEFORE THE NEW POLICIES

The service for local government (*chih-i*) was often mistakenly considered to be the same as the labor service (corvée, *li-i,* or *yao-i*), even by some Sung officials. The confusion arose principally because the labor service, which was much better known, was generally referred to simply as "service" (*i*).[1] Actually, the two kinds of service belonged to different categories. The labor service had long been obligatory upon all able-bodied persons as reported in the census registrations, unless they had been specifically exempted. Since the introduction of the two-tax system (*liang-shui-fa*) during the T'ang, it had been largely commuted into tax levies along with the land tax, although from time to time the people were still called upon to supply needed labor.

The service for local government had a different historical origin. During the Han period this service was the duty (*chih,* as in *chih-i*) of local leaders, who were selected from the population and duly appointed by the government in recognition of their proven ability and of public esteem for them. These country officers (*hsiang-kuan*) had an appreciable amount of social prestige and administrative authority in their own communities, under the supervision of the local government. The able ones, furthermore, were promoted by the government to the status of civil servants, and not a few reached the rank of minister. Unfortunately, through the centuries the position of these country officers deteriorated, owing to a number of factors: the growth of the bureaucracy through privilege, patronage, recommendations, and examinations; the monopoly of local government positions by the rising aristocratic clans during the Six Dynasties; the general increase of bureaucratic power over the people during the Sui and T'ang periods; and especially the usurpation of military power at the expense of all civilian jurisdiction toward the end of the T'ang and during the Five Dynasties. By the time of the Sung, even the term "country officers" was forgotten. Their place was taken by service personnel requisitioned and assigned by the local government; the service was no longer an honored duty, but a painful imposition often accompanied by humiliation and financial ruin.[2]

The vastness of the personnel servicing local government corresponded to that of the Sung bureaucracy. This service personnel may be classified into three groups: those performing guard duties, office duties, and village duties. The first group included office guards (yü-hou) and military servicemen at the magistrate's office (chiang-li ya-ch'ien); the latter was an exceptional group with the privilege of exemption from tax and from other services. The office personnel, both at the prefectural and subprefectural government offices, included many people. Best known among them were those collectively designated as the office servicemen (ya-ch'ien) who, under the immediate direction of the clerks, took care of revenue receipts, granary storage, transportation, office maintenance, office provisions, and a host of miscellaneous duties. In actuality, many had specific designations according to their respective duties; to mention but a few: bookkeepers (*tien-li*), scribes or copyists (*shu-piao-ssu*), guest-attendants (*k'e-ssu*), ushers (*t'ung-yin-kuan*), office hall attendants (*t'ing-tzu*), measurers (*tou-tzu*), transporters (*chieh-tzu*), storage watchmen (*k'u-tzu*), grain cleaners (*ch'ia-tzu*), office messengers (*ch'eng-fu*), laborers (*jen-li* and *shou-li*), miscellaneous servants (*san-ts'ung*). The office of a large prefectural government had more than a thousand such personnel. The total service personnel throughout the Sung empire must have been more than a million. In fact, government administration could not have functioned without them.[3]

The third group, those performing village duties, included village wardens (*li-cheng*), neighborhood leaders (*hu-chang*), and village scribes (*hsiang-shu-shou*). This group, after assisting in tax assessment, were mainly responsible for tax collection. In addition, there were village elders (*ch'i-chang*), bowmen (*kung-shou* or *kung-chien-shou*), and village guardsmen or militia (*chuang-ting*), who had policing duties.[4]

The most noteworthy of these groups was the office-duty personnel. They in turn were divided into two categories by their origins. Those who voluntarily applied for service in the local government office as a vocation were called long-term or career office servicemen (*ch'ang-ming ya-ch'ien*). They were unsalaried, receiving compensation for their services from the incomes of the government-supervised factories (*fang*, mainly distilleries), market gatherings (*ch'ang*), ferry tolls (*chin* or *chin-tu*), and the like. The other category did not volunteer to serve, but were requisitioned by the government. They were known as the office servicemen from the villages (*li-cheng ya-ch'ien* and *hsiang-hu ya-ch'ien*) or the requisitioned office servicemen.[5]

The conditions of these two categories of office servicemen

differed widely. The experienced career servicemen stood close to the clerks with a similar chance of earning, or illegally gaining, a comfortable income. The requisitioned servicemen, on the contrary, suffered a great deal. Many did not know their way about in the government offices, or how to render the services required of them; they were ignorant of how to bribe the clerks into helping them and giving them easier assignments, or how to avoid being deceived by the career servicemen. In fact, they were often given the heavier burdens and compelled to supply provisions for the social events, private entertainment, and personal luxuries of the insatiable officials.[6]

The endless miseries to which this group was subjected led to many evils. People would deliberately impoverish themselves or simulate poverty in the hope of evading service. They resorted to such evasions as cheating in registering property, failing to make census reports, and ostensibly, or even actually dividing the family into several separate households. Other devices were tragic: infanticide, suicide, or the marrying off of a widowed mother or widowed grandmother. Some simply fled, seeking a living in trade or handicrafts in the larger cities, or becoming monks or bandits.[7]

Such a situation could not continue to be ignored by the government. Fan Chung-yen in 1043 proposed the consolidation of local government units by reducing the number of prefectures and subprefectures, which in turn would reduce the amount of service imposition. This measure eliminated some 23,622 in service personnel, from a total of more than 1,000,000 in the whole nation. Similar efforts were made from time to time, but improvement on the whole was limited.[8] Han Ch'i introduced a minor reform known as the Five-Grade System (*Wu-teng-fa*) in 1051. The services were classified into five grades, according to the burden involved, and the people liable to assignment were also classified into five corresponding grades, according to their wealth. This minor reform relieved little suffering. As Ssu-ma Kuang pointed out, the wealthy families were still ruined by the requisitioned services, with the result that few cared to be rich. But Ssu-ma himself had no constructive remedy to offer.[9]

THE CONTROVERSY OVER THE HIRED SERVICE SYSTEM

Wang introduced a sweeping reform in the local government service. The system of requisitioning services by rotating assignment from among the relatively well-to-do families (Ch'ai-i-fa) was superseded by Wang's Hired Service System (Mu-i-fa). An experiment was first carried out at K'ai-feng, the capital, in 1069. The population was allowed to express its opinion, and the results of the experiment were judged satisfactory. At the same time, the service personnel in K'ai-feng alone was reduced by 830.[10] The K'ai-feng experiment, with due revision, became the law of the land in the tenth month of 1071. Its main features were the following:[11]

1. All households, including those not previously liable to the requisitioned service, paid a service exemption tax (mien-i-ch'ien) in cash.

2. The service exemption tax was governed by a graduated schedule that classified the village households into fifteen grades, according to a quinquennial survey of property; the households in the cities, which had previously rendered no service, were classified into ten grades, according to a triennial survey of property.

3. The households of bureaucratic families, households with only one male adult, no male adult, or no male at all,

and the temples — all previously exempted from service — paid half of the scheduled tax.

4. The tax included a 10 per cent surtax or "surplus tax" (k'uan-sheng-ch'ien). This was originally intended to cover possible tax arrears and deficits in times of exigency, but later it was actually used for other purposes in state financing — for instance, to give salaries to the clerks.

5. The service exemption tax, including the surtax, was payable twice a year, concurrently with the land tax.

6. From the tax received, the local government hired its own personnel, at fixed rates. Three kinds of hired service personnel were especially important: the office servicemen, who must first post a bond; the bowmen, who must pass an archery test; and the bookkeepers, who must pass a test in writing and accounting. Their terms of appointment were from two to three years.

7. The career servicemen originally at the office were retained, after some reduction in number, but they too were put on a salary basis. The local government itself, instead of the servicemen as heretofore, collected the incomes from the factories, market gatherings, ferry tolls, and the like, and used them to pay the servicemen.

8. The village duties, it is important to note, were neither commuted to tax payment nor put on a hired basis. Village elders were selected from among the households from the first to the third grade in the tax schedule, for a term of one year. Guard duty similarly rotated among the fourth- and fifth-grade households having two or more adults. Twice a year neighborhood leaders were selected from the fourth-grade households with both property and adults, for the short term of each tax payment. A subsequent reform in 1074 abolished the neighborhood leaders and replaced them by tax-collecting unit leaders (ts'ui-shui chia-t'ou); by then the tithing system

had organized the neighborhood population into such units (*chia*), comprising twenty to thirty families each.[12] In short, the village duties remained as requisitioned services.

9. At first the service exemption tax was collected rigorously. Later some areas, on the plea of exceptional circumstances, were permitted by the central government to postpone collection or to cancel the tax for a limited period.[13]

The Hired Service System encountered strenuous opposition and violent denunciations from innumerable officials. Among them were such outstanding conservative and moderate leaders as Ssu-ma Kuang, Chang Fang-p'ing (1007–1091), Han Ch'i, Su Shih, his brother Su Ch'e, Yang Hui (1027–1088), and Liu Chih. Their various arguments are summarized in the following paragraphs.[14]

First, the antireformers opposed the Hired Service System in principle on the following grounds:

1. It imposed an additional tax burden on all people and thereby set a bad precedent (Su Shih, Su Ch'e, and Liu).

2. The surtax in the service exemption tax was most unreasonable. It was collected on the pretext of covering possible arrears and deficits, yet it was used for many other purposes. The expanding state finance meant nothing but the cheating and exploiting of the people (Han and Su Ch'e).

3. The amount of the service exemption tax was determined by the central government according to a unified plan, and a definite amount was assigned to each local government unit, with little regard for regional differences and local conditions (Yang and Liu).

4. The tax payment in cash created a currency scarcity or "cash famine" (*ch'ien-huang*). All the farmers, in order to get cash for tax payments, had to sell their products at the same time, thus causing a fall in prices to their disadvantage. Nor did the farmers, long accustomed to a self-sufficient

household economy, know much about market operations or the ways of money economy. Many were thus ruined (Ssu-ma, Yang, Liu, and Chang).

5. The antireform leaders believed that the former service personnel, requisitioned from relatively well-to-do families, were trustworthy, while the hired personnel were unreliable. The latter were willing to be hired because they had no stable vocation. Since they commanded little respect in the community, their services could not possibly be as good or effective. They had to be given a sufficiently high pay to induce them to apply for service, yet they often ran away upon default (Ssu-ma, Su Ch'e, Chang, Liu, and Yang).

In addition to these general considerations, the antireform leaders made specific criticisms of the service exemption tax, its administration and its rating schedule:

1. The survey that determined the grades of tax liability was not reliable (Liu).

2. Officials eager to please the central government and to show their pretended administrative ability deliberately put many households into the upper grades where they did not belong and thus collected far more tax than was necessary (Ssu-ma, Liu, Chang, and Han).

3. The tax schedule was too inflexible. It provided for neither cancellation nor any other measure that might be desirable in case of famine and other hardships (Liu, Chang, and Han).

4. The tax burden was unwise and unfair. It did not necessarily relieve the upper-grade households, as they had formerly assumed service only by rotation. On the other hand, the burden now also fell upon the poor, who had had no such burden before (all the antireform leaders).

5. Those who were previously exempted from the burden of requisitioned service should remain exempted. The house-

holds with one male adult, no male adult, or no male at all deserved sympathy. The temples should also receive consideration. The government should realize that on many occasions and in times of need it relied upon numerous contributions from the urban population, especially from the merchants and traders. It was therefore reasonable to exempt them from the requisitioned services and unreasonable to impose on them the service exemption tax. Likewise, families of the bureaucrats should have the privilege of exemption (all the anti-reform leaders).

Confronted with these complaints, Wang asked Tseng Pu, who had been mainly responsible for drafting the Hired Service regulations, to make pointed replies. Tseng did not attempt to defend the new system on the level of the principles involved. The differences of opinion here were fundamental, and since the Emperor had already approved these principles a defense was unnecessary. Tseng confined himself to the specific criticisms of the rates and the administration of the service exemption tax, point by point:[15]

1. The survey that determined the grades of tax liability was as reliable as, if not more reliable than, previous surveys made in connection with the land tax.

2. No case had been reported of the officials' deliberately collecting a higher amount of tax than was intended by the government. If such cases occurred, it was the fault of the officials, who misunderstood or abused the system, and not of the system itself. An order was later issued to dismiss any official guilty of such a mistake.[16]

3. While the tax schedule did not provide for cancellation or other emergency measures during times of hardship, it must be recalled that the government would need these services all the time. Furthermore, the former requisitioned service system had allowed for no flexibility whatsoever.

4. While the scheduled taxes of the upper-grade households were sizable, each of these households paid for only a small portion of the entire service required by the government in any given year. This burden was not nearly so disastrous as that under the requisitioned service system, where a family could easily be ruined by having to furnish the entire service for the whole year when its turn came.[17]

5. Since the services were for the local government, it was only fair that the burden should be shared by all the households in that area. Those previously exempted should no longer have such a privilege. The urban population was able to make its complaints heard, thus giving an exaggerated impression of its suffering.[18]

The Hired Service System prevailed, over the objections of the antireformers. Its results, so far as state finance was concerned, proved impressive.[19] However, the opposition and complaints persisted. When the anti-reform phase began the issue was reopened. Some reformers like Chang Ch'un admitted that the system had many faults and should be improved upon without being totally rescinded. Some mild conservatives, like Fan Ch'un-jen and Lü Kung-chu, and especially the southwestern moderate elements, notably the Su brothers and Lü T'ao, agreed that the system should be abolished, but gradually and carefully. But such determined conservatives as Liu Chih and Wang Yen-shou insisted that it should be categorically rescinded at once. Ssu-ma Kuang, the head of the antireform administration, generally agreed with this group, and an abrupt change was brought about, which was neither a total abolition of the Hired Service System, nor a total restoration of the former system. The principal changes were: the local government first hired the service personnel; when more help was needed, it requisitioned the services from the upper-grade households; these households in turn were permitted to hire other people to render the services assigned to them, while they themselves remained responsible.[20]

This modified system of requisitioned service proved unsatisfactory to many people. Furthermore, without the tax revenues of the Hired Service System the state finance suffered from mounting deficits. In the postreform phase the Hired Service System was abruptly revived and the tax burden became even heavier than it had been originally in the reform phase.[21] It is highly significant that, despite the notorious maladministration of the postreform and the objections of the conservative scholars, local government service during the Southern Sung was supplied mainly according to the hired system. In short, this particular reform of Wang's became an established institution of the subsequent Chinese empires.

THE SIGNIFICANT FEATURES OF THE NEW POLICIES
AS SEEN IN THE HIRED SERVICE SYSTEM

The partisan attacks and counterattacks and the abrupt changes back and forth have obscured for historians the significant features of the Hired Service System. Since this system was central to the New Policies program, its salient features must reflect those of the New Policies as a whole.

The first significant feature of the Hired Service System was its commutation to cash tax payment. This indicates a preference for a money economy in the state finance under the New Policies. The system worked better in the southern areas where money economy was better developed; it caused considerable hardship in the northern areas. Generally speaking, the New Policies received comparatively more support among the southern areas, but encountered strenuous opposition among the northern areas.[22]

Secondly, the Hired Service System was an integral part of an effective system of state financing and it should be evaluated in conjunction with other related measures. An urgent reason for the inauguration of the system was the expenditures occasioned by the military campaign near the border of the Hsi Hsia kingdom.[23] Funds were also needed for other purposes — for example, to give salaries to the local government clerks.[24] This does not mean, however, that the New Policies aimed only at increasing the revenues without cutting down the expenditures. In fact, efforts were made from time to time to reduce the number of prefectures and subprefectures and also the number of tributes and their transportation, with the intention of lessening the amount of local government service in particular and of effecting government economy in general.[25]

An important feature of this effective state financing was the management of currency.[26] More coins were minted in order to meet the demand for cash caused by the cash tax payment required under the Hired Service System and by the generally expanded state finance under the New Policies. Yet no inflation took place. In fact, the reform phase was a time of deflation and low prices.[27] No evidence indicates that the deflation was a result of planning. A variety of circumstances was responsible for it.

On the one hand, with the removal of the legal ban on private handling of copper, a certain amount of currency went to other countries, such as the Liao Empire, Korea, and Japan. Some coins were reconverted into copper for manufacturing purposes. Meanwhile, the heavy taxation drew a large quantity of currency back to the government treasury.

On balance, there was probably no significant increase in the volume of currency in active circulation.

On the other hand, years of good harvest made for an abundant supply of commodities. General prosperity prevailed. A number of New Policy measures also helped to stabilize prices. Under these circumstances, the low prices benefited not only the consumers in general but the state itself to a great extent. Though the state took in many revenues in kind, it still had to buy much more in order to meet all its needs. The state was therefore the largest buyer or consumer in the market. With plenty of money from cash tax payment when the money had high value in terms of low prices, the state must have acquired through this effective financing an enviable amount of purchasing power.

The third feature of the Hired Service System was its heavy tax burden. The glaring defects of the requisitioned service system were obvious when upper-grade households assigned to service were reduced to poverty within a year. But the miseries caused by the tax which supported the Hired Service System, while not nearly so apparent, were certainly more widespread and far-reaching.[28] The mounting banditry in the northern and some other areas, though due mainly to famines, was in part traceable to heavy taxation.[29] And heavy taxation was typical of the New Policies program, whatever the merits of its effective state financing.

Fourthly, the Hired Service System accentuated class inequality. Despite the violent disagreement between the reformers and the antireformers, both groups in effect helped to lighten the burden of the upper-grade households. The Hired Service System spread the burden down to the poor; the antireform policy allowed upper-grade households to spend less than before in hiring substitutes to render service to the government for them. Also, the wealthy who loaned money to those who lacked cash with which to pay the tax under the system stood to gain in a period of currency scarcity and deflation. On the other hand, during the antireform phase bureaucratic families once again enjoyed exemption from service. During the postreform, many bureaucratic families evaded the restored tax payment in lieu of service, as it was not rigidly enforced by the corrupt administration. By the Southern Sung period exemption and tax evasion on the part of the bureaucratic families had become even more pronounced.[30] The charge of class inequality, as seen in the Hired Service System from its beginning to the time of the Southern Sung, is also generally applicable to the New Policies program. Wang, in principle, placed the interests of the state before those of any particular class. Among the classes, he probably intended to help the relatively poor, who were the majority of the population, rather than the rich. But there was plenty of room for the influential and the wealthy to manipulate the New Policies program to their own advantage.[31] Wang's policies tended to favor consumers in general and small merchants to a degree, while making numerous efforts to curb the interests of the monopolistic merchants. But whatever progress the New Policies made toward the realization of these objectives was largely offset by the heavy taxation, which did fall upon the majority of the people.

Finally, the Hired Service System helped to expand the clerical subbureaucracy in local government. The hired service personnel now joined the clerks in such great numbers that they became in effect a part of the clerical subbureaucracy. There was little effective supervision over either the hired service personnel or the clerks, especially in their corrupt collusion with upper-grade and bureaucratic families. This is again typical of the New Policies program. While the government expanded the scope of its operations, it needed a larger number of clerical and service personnel to carry out these operations, and it could hardly avoid giving these personnel a larger share of responsibility, as well as more opportunities for abuse, than they had ever had before.

These five features of the Hired Service System constituted the basis for the criticisms raised against the New Policies as a whole. However, the conservatives who had opposed the New Policies proved even more helpless when they came to power. They opposed the Hired Service System, for they believed that the heavy tax payment involved contributed to the rise of banditry, which threatened the property of large landowners. They abolished this system, partly because it was based on a money economy which they disliked. In restoring the prereform system they were in effect at a loss as to how to devise a more adequate policy. Their limited concept of state financing was mainly to reduce government expenditures, but they were unable even to raise sufficient funds to meet the needs after the reduction. In this instance, as in many others, the conservatives' incompetence in statecraft and the inadequacy of their conventional Confucian ideas were altogether too apparent. By comparison, the New Policies, even though they failed to achieve their intended objectives but not for the reasons given by the conservatives — still deserve considerable respect for having attempted to deal realistically with the increasingly acute problems of tax burden and state finance in an expanding money economy.

VII

Conclusion

This reappraisal has shown Wang An-shih as a bureaucratic idealist who upheld the ideal of a professionally well-trained and administratively well-controlled bureaucracy as the principal instrument for the realization of a Confucian moral society. It has also described him as an institutional reformer, who endeavored not only to change government institutions but also to found new ones in order to guide and shape the behavior of both bureaucrats and the people. Wang's principal emphasis was not upon the promulgation and enforcement of law. Nor did he believe the objective of "enriching the state and strengthening the army" to be of prime importance. His ultimate goal was to improve the social customs of the people, looking toward a perfect social order. For these reasons, he and those who agreed with him at the time, as well as those who admired him in later centuries, denied that he was a Legalist. However, the majority of conventional Confucianists believed that the emphasis should be placed upon individual officials rather than upon the bureaucracy. To them, what Wang meant by regulatory systems — or in our words, government institutions and government-initiated institutions — were of the same nature as law. Consequently, they considered Wang a Legalist or at least a misguided Confucianist who had strayed in the same direction as the Legalists. In all fairness, in terms of the theoretical justifications upon which Wang based his views and in terms of his ultimate goal of a moral society, we may still regard Wang as essentially a Confucianist. He was of course a radical Confucianist, but radical only in comparison with many conservative Confucianists.

Since his idealism was basically bureaucratic, Wang always put the interests of the state, as he interpreted them, above everything else. He did not develop a clear definition of his objectives in terms of their effects upon the various social classes. He thought he was helping the majority of the population; yet the improvement of the state finances which the New Policies brought about was probably far greater than the benefits they brought to the people. While the bureaucratic families and large landowners complained about some features of the New Policies that were objectionable to them, many medium-sized landowners and other less well-to-do people had their share of complaints on other grounds. In short, Wang's policy was neither clearly nor firmly built upon a well-defined social basis.

In Wang's view the bureaucracy was especially important. Yet, precisely on this point he failed, for he did not obtain strong enough support from the bureaucrats. He did not even succeed in inspiring a sustaining loyalty among the executive type of bureaucrats, upon whom he depended principally to carry out the New Policies. What the New Policies did achieve was lost when some of these bureaucrats degenerated into the manipulative type. Furthermore, Wang was theoretical in policy matters rather than practical in politics. He gave far more attention to administration than to the winning over of his opponents, as for example, of the southwestern moderates, who opposed him less vehemently than did the northern conservatives. Thus, though he emphasized the importance of the bureacracy, he did not really carry the support of the bureaucracy at all.

The bureaucracy performed its service through the government's operations and here Wang's program ran into additional difficulties: growing absolutism, increasing centralization with its attendant danger of power manipulation, greater conformity which was neither politically nor administratively desirable, and the gradually expanding but ever incorrigible clerical subbureaucracy which did not carry out the policies as intended. From the reform, through the antireform, to the postreform, these difficulties became steadily greater, to a degree never anticipated by Wang.

China was a bureaucratic state. Wang was indeed outstanding, if not exceptional, in his emphasis upon utilitarian statecraft, upon the bureaucracy, and upon the government institutions and government-initiated institutions. Since his approach did not succeed, the only alternative seemed to be that of conventional Confucianism or what, from the Southern Sung period on, was respected as orthodox Confucianism. Yet this latter approach stressed the moral qualities and the moral influence of the bureaucratic class and disregarded utilitarian policies and manipulative attitudes toward the state machinery.

One cannot help asking whether such a moralistic approach was sufficiently realistic. Did it not gloss over the facts of life in a bureaucratic state and thereby inhibit later Chinese thinking about political institutions?

NOTES

INDEX

Notes

CHAPTER I.

A Brief Account of Wang's Life and the New Policies

1. The translation New Laws comes from the Chinese term, *hsin-fa. Fa* means laws; but it also means methods or measures. Sometimes *fa* is used as a simplified expression meaning *fa-chih,* which may be translated as "systems established by the laws." For a full discussion of this point, see Chapter III under "Wang's political and economic theories."

2. Full accounts of Wang's life may be found in several well-known works. In Chinese, K'e, *Wang;* Liang, *Wang;* Teng, *Wang;* and Ts'ai, *Wang,* the latter containing the most substantial research. In Japanese, Saeki, *Wang.* The most frequently used work in English is Williamson, *Wang An-shih.*

3. The translations of many Chinese terms in Williamson are not always satisfactory. Whenever desirable, I suggest new translations. For the names of government offices and official titles, I have generally followed Kracke, *Civil Service* and *Civil Service Titles.*

4. The Chinese terms for these reform measures, numbered as in the text, are: 1. Chih-chih San-ssu T'iao-li Ssu; 2. *Ch'ing-miao Ch'ien;* 3. *Chün-shu;* 4. *Mu-i Fa;* 5. *Pao-chia;* 6. *Fang-t'ien Chün-shui;* 7. Same as 5; 8. *Pao-ma Fa* and Chün-ch'i-chien; 9. *T'ung-pi* or simply *ch'ien;* 10. *Shih-i Fa;* 11. *Mien-hang Ch'ien;* 12. T'ai-hsüeh and chou-hsüeh; 13. *Ts'e, lun, ching-i, shih,* and *fu;* 14. *Pao-jen* or sponsored appointment; 15. *Li* or *hsü-li.* The system whereby the clerks were paid a salary and their misconduct was punished more severely than before was called the Granary System or *Ts'ang Fa,* for many clerks had duties connected with granaries; also, a large portion of their salaries came from granaries. Granary here is a general term referring to both the granaries and the local government treasuries (see Chapter V in "The

clerical subbureaucracy"). For general accounts of these reform measures, see any of the well-known works given in Note 2, or in the collection of material on the Northern Sung referred to as CPPM, 66:1–18, and 68:1–75:21.

5. The most convenient primary sources on the reform, the antireform, and the postreform phases are found in the CPPM. Besides those sections cited in Note 4, see 59:1–61:16; 63:1–64:10; 94:1–98:17; 100:1–102:18; 108:1–110:15; 120:1–122:16; 124:1–8; and 129:1–131:22.

CHAPTER II.

Problems of Interpretation

1. Though the *Shih-lu* itself is no longer extant, many of its materials have found their way into HCP, SHY, the best primary sources on the Northern Sung, and YYCA, a collection of early Sung biographies.

2. CYYL (an annual history since the beginning of the Southern Sung), 40:745, 46:831; CCTSC (Ch'ao's bibliographical notes), 2a:15–16, 2c:19. See also Ts'ai, 25:1–6; Liang, 10–13; K'e, *Wang*, 381–385; Williamson, II, 60–70.

3. TKIL (notes of Tseng Pu), 9:69; SS (Sung dynastic history), 329:5263; CPPM, 113:1–10.

4. Consult Toyama, "Conservatives and progressives."

5. CTYL (classified comments of Chu Hsi), 127:13–14; SS, 243:5161. See also SS, 471:5676, 242:5160, 243:5162.

6. Ts'ai, preface:2, considers HCP prejudiced. There is some doubt, however, whether Ts'ai actually studied HCP with care (see Yang, *Wang*, 2:2). Okazaki, "Wang's domestic policy," pp. 175–178, points out that Ts'ai often quotes the commentaries on Wang's poems that are favorable to Wang. These commentaries were written by Li Pi, the son of Li T'ao, who compiled HCP. Moreover, HCP corresponds closely with SHY. Evidently, Li T'ao in compiling HCP confined his editorial alterations to a minimum (see Kracke, *Civil Service*, p. 240).

7. Ts'ai, preface; Liang, pp. 9–10; K'e, *Wang*, pp. 385–392; Williamson, II, 27–29.

8. Yang, *Wang*, 1:12–22; K'e, *Wang*, pp. 403–410; Williamson, II, 69 and 118–120. It should be noted that SS draws heavily upon the words and conduct of the famous officials by Chu Hsi, referred to as MCYHL. For a critical evaluation of the reliability of MCYHL, see Miyazaki, "Literary class," pp. 139–140.

9. YS (Yüan dynasty history) 182:6548–6549. The chief compilers of SS were Ou-yang Hsüan and Chang Chi-yen (see KCWC (collected works of Ou-yang Hsüan), 13:5–7, 16:11). A contributor who probably disagreed with the two chief compilers was Yüan Chüeh (see the works of Yüan Chüeh, referred to as CYCSC, 18:7, 41:12–13, 41:13–19).

10. A probable fabrication is the essay entitled "Pien chien lun" (Essay on identifying the villain). Allegedly it was written by Su Hsün, the father of both Su Shih and Su Ch'e, to denounce Wang An-shih. Actually, Su Hsün never wrote it. See Ts'ai, 10:1–13; Liang, pp. 95–98; K'e, *Wang*, pp. 389–391; Williamson, II, 109–110 and 148–157. It may be added that fabrications claiming to be exposé literature had appeared before and during Wang's time (see the encyclopedia of historical institutions, referred to as TK, pp. 1767–1768, and Liu, "Northern Sung political struggle").

11. Hsiao, 2:143–67; de Bary, "Neo-Confucianism."

12. Liang, pp. 155–194, 205–226.

13. Ferguson, "Wang"; Liang, p. 1; K'e, *Wang*, pp. 427–428; Williamson, II, 182. Otto Franke and Richard Wilhelm, in their general histories of China, follow similar interpretations.

14. Review of Lin, *Gay Genius*, by Nieh Ch'ung-ch'i, in *Yenching hsüeh-pao*, 34:298 ff. (Peking, 1948).

15. Wang, "Preface to reform," pp. 533–546; Naitō, pp. 123–130; Sudō, *Bureaucratic landholdings*, pp. 5–77; Nakamura, "Power of Wang," pp. 1–12; Ikeda, "Tithing system," pp. 7–8. The last article contains a brief classification of the various interpretations of Wang. Saeki, *Wang*, a Japanese publication in 1941, and Teng, *Wang*, the most recent book on Wang, published in Chinese in 1953 for popular reading, both follow the viewpoints of recent research.

16. Wang, "Preface to reform," pp. 533–546.

17. See Chapter III, in "The differences between reformers and conservatives."

18. Liu, "Fan Chung-yen," pp. 126–130.

19. Kracke, "Sung Society." This account of Sung society before Wang's time is preferable to that in Williamson, II, 71–97.

20. Sogabe, *Finance*, pp. 22–37, 68–69.

21. Hsiao, 2:143–197; de Bary, "Neo-Confucianism," pp. 110–111.

22. Liu, "Mei Yao-chen."

CHAPTER III.

Wang and the Political Thought of the Northern Sung

1. Hsiao, 2:143–145; Ch'ien, 1:2–25; Ho, "Geographic distribution of scholarship," 352–360. For example, the philosopher Chou Tun-i was far less famed as a scholar than Wang An-shih; see Ts'ai, 8:9 and *tsa-lu* (appendix), 1:7–8.

2. Chang, "Southern China society," pp. 39–40; Ch'ien, *Neo-Confucianism*, 1:1–8; and Takeuchi, "Sung learning," p. 15. According to Chu Hsi, the details of Hu Yüan's teaching method were no longer known to the Southern Sung scholars (see CTYL, 129:7). For the part played by the two scholars, Hu Yüan and Sun Fu, in the reform of 1043–1044, consult Fischer, "Fan Chung-yen," and Liu, "Fan Chung-yen."

3. Mou, "Ch'un-ch'iu study," pp. 113–117; Takeuchi, "Sung learning," pp. 27–30; Ho, "Geographic distribution of scholarship," p. 347. Hu Yüan and Sun Fu did not like each other (see CTYL, 129:6–7).

4. Ch'ien, 1:9–12; Hsiao, 2:145–149; HCP, 237:8.

5. Morohashi, "Li Kou." The works of Li Kou were posthumously presented to the Emperor by the reform leaders in 1074 (see HCP, 254:9).

6. Ho, "Geographic distribution of scholarship," p. 365; Aoyama, "Kiangsi bureaucrats," pp. 24–37; Sudō, *Bureaucratic landholdings*, pp. 9–76 and 144–152.

7. Hsiao, 2:181–189; Ho, "Geographic distribution of scholarship," pp. 352–353, 374.

8. Hsiao, 2:170–178; Ch'ien, 1:22–33; Lin, *Gay Genius, passim*; Takeuchi, "Sung learning," pp. 27–28; and CTYL, 129:7, 130:-14–19.

9. Miyazaki, "Literary class," pp. 139–169; Liu, "Northern Sung political struggle," pp. 104–107.

10. Liu, "Fan Chung-yen," pp. 126–130.

11. LCWC (collected works of Wang An-shih), 84:10–11; K'e, *Wang*, pp. 216–238. The Lo School, though conservative, differed from the Shuo School in attaching considerable value to the study of both *Chou-li* and *Mencius*.

12. Mou, "*Ch'un-ch'iu* study," pp. 170–172; Morohashi, *Confucianism*, pp. 145–160; Takeuchi, "Sung learning," pp. 27–30. See also K'e, *Wang*, pp. 230–236.

13. The charge that Wang An-shih slighted the *Ch'un-ch'iu* as "worthless fragments of government chronicles" is an exaggeration but not entirely without basis. Ts'ai, in defending Wang, overstates his case; and both K'e and Williamson follow Ts'ai. See Ts'ai, 11:3–11; K'e, *Wang*, pp. 230–234; Williamson, II, 313–316. It is true that Wang sometimes mentioned *Ch'un-ch'iu* with due respect in his writings and even wrote a commentary on *Tso-chuan*. In the final analysis, however, Wang did cast grave doubts on *Ch'un-ch'iu* as well as the three *chuan*; see LCWC, 72:1–5; Yang, *Wang*, 2:22; HCP, 247:11–12.

14. Morohashi, *Confucianism*, pp. 145–160. On the controversy over *Mencius*, see Hsia, pp. 56–79; CCTSC, 3a:9, 5c:28, 5c:45–46, and *hou-chih* (supplementary notes), 2:1.

15. Hsiao, 2:168–170 and 178–181; and Ch'en, pp. 9–19.

16. Suzuki, "Sung buddhism."

17. CCTSC, 1c:16; K'e, *Wang*, pp. 213–215; Williamson, I, 367 and 373; II, 54, 201 and 250.

18. HCP, 233:14, 275:11; LCWC, 83:2–4 and 7–8. Wang's relation to Taoism was relatively indirect; see LCWC, 83:5, 8 and 10. For Wang's poems and their affinity to Buddhism, see Hu, p. 56; LCWC, 3:15–30; Williamson, II, 292. Also consult Wright, "Buddhism and Chinese Culture."

19. LCCSI (supplement to the works of Wang An-shih), p. 37.

20. HCP, 279:11; LCWC, 43:22–23.

21. LCCSI, p. 5.

22. LCWC, 3:15–21; see also Williamson, II, 291–292.

23. Sudō, *Bureaucratic landholdings*, pp. 9–76.

24. Nishi, "Three literati," pp. 30–52; Sogabe, *Finance*, pp. 6–7. On Wang's political theory of "entrusting the officials" with a greater amount of authority and giving them longer tenure of office, see LCWC, 39:83, 41:5–6, 41:8–9, and 63:73–74. Wang's efforts in carrying out this theory were denounced by Sssu-ma Kuang as "trespassing upon the proper jurisdiction of other offices"; see Ts'ai, 9:6–9; Liang, pp. 120–121; K'e, *Wang*, pp. 359–366; Williamson, I, 154–156.

25. Sudō, *Bureaucratic landholdings*, pp. 9–76; Aoyama, "Kiangsi bureaucrats," pp. 19–37.

26. LCWC, 71:85–87, 74:18–19, 77:53. Wang claimed that his family owned "no land" at all. This may have been a slight literary exaggeration. The fact remains that his family did depend heavily on his salary; consult Ts'ai, 4:14 ff.; Williamson, I, 20 and 41.

27. Sudō, *Bureaucratic landholdings*, pp. 86–90; Aoyama, "Kiangsi bureaucrats," pp. 25–32. See also LCWC, 88:45–47, 90:68–69, 92:77–80, 92:84–85, 93:86–88. The last citation, incidentally, concerns the family relation between Wang and the Tseng brothers, Tseng Kung and Tseng Pu.

28. Chang, "Southern China society," pp. 40–41; Higashi, "Wang's agrarian system," pp. 193–194; Sudō, *Land system*, pp. 474–480.

29. Ch'üan, "Natural economy," pp. 170–173; Ch'üan, "Public revenue," pp. 189–221; Wang, *Economic history*, 1–11.

30. Sogabe, *Finance*, pp. 30–37, 68–69, 153–161; Ch'üan, "Public revenue," pp. 189–221. See also Liang, pp. 114 ff.; K'e, *Wang*, pp. 61–65; Williamson, I, 113–120.

31. Ch'üan, "Price fluctuations," pp. 357–375.

32. Shikimori, "State trade," pp. 24–27; Ch'üan, "Export and import trade," pp. 272–274; Sogabe, *Finance*, 22–27.

33. For convenient examples of the conservatives' criticism and Wang's defense, see Liang, pp. 111–112 and 121–122; K'e, *Wang*, pp. 67–68 and 84–87; Williamson, I, 105–106 and 162–163.

34. Ch'üan, "Export and import trade," pp. 273–274, 296–298; Ch'üan, "Officials and private trade," pp. 204–248; T'ao, "Eco-

nomic problems," pp. 85–86; Wang, "Preface to reform," p. 584. See also HCP, 262:30.

35. LCWC, 67:53–54; Williamson, II, 325–327. In this note and many others immediately following, the reference indicates that Williamson has translated the same items, though in a number of instances not necessarily the exact passages. His translations are generally too liberal and sometimes inaccurate.

36. LCWC, 69:74–75; Williamson, I, 114–117.

37. LCWC, 66:40–41; Williamson, II, 335–338.

38. LCWC, 83:3–4.

39. LCWC, 66:43; Williamson, II, 362.

40. LCWC, 64:18.

41. Ibid., 39:79; also repeated at 41:1–2. The first citation is the "Wan-yen-shu" (Myriad word memorial), a translation of which is in Williamson, I, 48–84. A much improved translation by Professor Ch'ü T'ung-tsu will soon become available in Sources on Chinese Tradition, edited by Wm. Theodore de Bary of Columbia University.

42. LCWC, 84:10–11.

43. Ibid., 67:51–52. See also ibid., 73:17–18; Williamson, I, 367.

44. LCWC, 83:4.

45. Ibid., 66:45–46; Williamson, II, 340–342. See also LCWC, 66:46–47; Williamson, II, 344–345.

46. LCWC, 67:52–53.

47. Ibid., 41:8, 67:52–53, 71:94, 75:35, 76:39–40, 83:3–4.

48. Ibid., 84:16; Williamson, II, 290–291.

49. LCWC, 73:17–18; Williamson, I, 367.

50. LCWC, 39:79–92; Williamson, I, 48–84. See Note 41.

51. Ch'ü, Law and Society, pp. 241 ff.

52. Saeki, "Heavy penalty places," pp. 507–508.

53. LCWC, 72:8–9, 39:80; K'e, Wang, pp. 43–47; Araki, "Prohibition de cuivre," pp. 24–25; Saeki, "Heavy penalty places," p. 523.

54. LCWC, 69:69; Williamson, II, 372–374.

55. LCWC, 69:21–22; Williamson, I, 330–336.

56. LCWC, 82:93; and Williamson, I, 86–87.

57. LCCSI, pp. 18–20.

58. LCWC, 69:21–22; Williamson, I, 330–336.

59. LCWC, 62:3–8.

60. Williamson, II, 233–36 and 240–242, the biographies of Sang Hung-yang and Liu Yen respectively. See also Ch'üan, "Natural economy," pp. 73–173, on the response of Lin Yen to the rise of money economy during his time.

61. Liu, "Fan Chung-yen," pp. 116–117.

62. LCWC, 70:81; Williamson, I, 118–120.

63. LCWC, 75:33–34; Williamson, I, 87.

64. LCWC, 70:79; Williamson, I, 300–301.

65. LCWC, 73:13; Williamson, I, 162–164.

66. LCWC, 73:12, Williamson, I, 154–156.

67. LCWC, 69:75; Williamson, I, 117.

68. LCWC, 4:29; Williamson, I, 122.

69. LCWC, 70:79–80. See also Yoshida, "Salt tax," pp. 416–421. Yoshida's discussion on Wang's attitude on salt trade and monopoly points out the complexity of such economic issues. Wang's economic thought still awaits more definitive study.

70. Ts'ai, tsa-lu (appendix), 1:1–3; Yang, Wang, 1:6–8; Liang, pp. 101–102; Williamson, I, 174 and 234; II, 140. The Emperor and Wang, though agreeing most of the time, had occasional disagreements (see TKIL, 9:74).

71. Yang, Wang, 2:12–13; CPPM, 63:1–64:10.

72. HCP, 221:17.

73. Ibid., 213:3, 213:6, 215:3, 221:17, 223:19, 224:10, 229:17, 234:16, 242:4, 242:16, 263:24, 264:20, 275:12. See also Notes 74 and 75.

74. HCP, 243:10.

75. Ibid., 250:12–13.

76. Yang, Wang, 2:7–9.

77. HCP, 215:3.

78. Ibid., 254:11, 265:73.

79. Ibid., 248:17–20, 251:4; CPPM, 75:13–17.

80. HCP, 247:1, 247:5, 254:11.

81. Ibid., 214:17 ff. See also Saeki, "Heavy penalty places," pp. 522–530; CPPM, 75:17–19.

82. HCP, 251:23, 252:2.

83. Ibid., 254:11, 254:19.

84. K'e, Wang, pp. 302–303, 339 ff.; Williamson, II, 1–5.

85. CCTSC, 1a:12.

86. CTYL, 128:18. See also Nishi, "Three literati."
87. HCP, 214:14; CTYL, 130:2; and CPPM, 66:1–7.
88. HCP, 242:1.
89. Sogabe, *Finance*, p. 153.
90. Yang, *Wang*, 2:7–9; Sogabe, *Finance*, pp. 24–25; Nieh, "Local government service," pp. 213–218.
91. HCP, 232:2, 236:26, 248:17–19, 254:10, 255:9, 256:4, 257:12–13, 261:9–11, 262:3–4, 266:6. See also Chao, p. 266; and Note 92.
92. HCP, 217:13–15, 220:15, 221:10; and CPPM, 85:1–88:12.
93. HCP, 218:6–7, 233:6, 235:14, 246:13–14, 262:3, 275:3, 279:13–14; Ikeda, "Tithing system"; CPPM, 71:1–14, 109:1–8.

CHAPTER IV.

The New Policies and the Behavior of the Bureaucrats

1. Miyazaki, "Literary class."
2. HCP, 108:18, 110:3; CPPM, 42:13–16; Chao I, p. 330.
3. Miyazaki, "Student life," pp. 638–645; Miyazaki, "Luxury," pp. 27–50; Ch'üan, "Officials and private trade," pp. 202–223. For the case of Ch'ang I, see HCP, 245:8.
4. Miyazaki, "Literary class," p. 163.
5. HCP, 226:13.
6. Ch'üan, "Price fluctuations," p. 388.
7. Miyazaki, "Local clerks," p. 15.
8. HCP, 273:7; Miyazaki, "Local clerks," pp. 22–27; Miyazaki, "Student life," p. 103.
9. HCP, 236:6.
10. *Ibid.*, 213:9, 214:8. See also the anthology of Sung anecdotes referred to as SPLC, 4:30.
11. HCP, 252:3–4; Ch'üan, "Officials and private trade," pp. 248:252.
12. HCP, 251:18, 218:5; CTYL, 129:9; and Miyazaki, "Literary class," pp. 151–152 respectively.
13. Sudō, *Bureaucratic landholdings*, p. 77.
14. HCP, 216:2.

15. CTYL, 130:4.

16. Miyazaki, "Local clerks," p. 20.

17. CTYL, 130:3; HCP, 248:9, 253:10, 255:3–4.

18. HCP, 214:13.

19. *Ibid.*, 226:7, 237:6; SPLC, 2:51.

20. Liang, p. 236; Okazaki, "Wang's domestic policy," pp. 179–180; Ts'ai, 4:7–8. See also LCWC, 77:52. Wang had a close friend named Wang Fung-yüan whose retiring mode of living was precisely of this description; see Kuo, 1:7–8.

21. HCP, 251:23.

22. *Ibid.*, 5:7–8; CTYL, 129:4–5; CPPM, 38:9–11.

23. Lü Hui-ch'ing, after Wang's first departure from the court, plotted to weaken Wang's influence. When Wang returned to power, he seemed displeased with Lü (see HCP, 259:1–2, 259:8, 261:9–10, 265:4, 265:24–28, 268:4–8). Other officials began to attack Lü (see HCP, 264:20–22, 266:10–12). Lü was dismissed from the court when he became implicated in a case of corruption on the part of his relatives (see HCP, 268:12–17, 269:3–8, 269:12, 269:16–17, 271:11, 275:7–8, 276:4–6, 276:9). Not long after Lü had gone, Wang himself went into permanent retirement with a high honorary title (see HCP, 280:5–6, 280:22–23, 281:8).

Wang never forgave Tseng Pu, another close associate at the beginning of the reform, for having contradicted him in the controversy over the State Trade System and the Guild Exemption Tax (see CPPM, 72:1–14). He refused to recall Tseng to the court after Lü's dismissal (see HCP, 251:28–29, 252:1–2, 252:11, 252:19, 253:9, 263:28, 264:4, 264:18). Thus depriving himself of several associates, Wang had to rely upon relatively inexperienced subordinates, and less trustworthy ones, like Teng Chien. He was soon to regret this; see HCP, 264:24, 266:16, 271:5; CPPM, 64:1–10.

24. Yang, *Wang*, 1:33–35; CTYL, 130:12, 130:28–29.

25. HCP, 237:8; Ts'ai, 3:3 and 7, 5:7–8; Williamson, I, 23–29; LCWC, 76:42–43.

26. HCP, 213:4–5.

27. *Ibid.*, 214:8 and 13.

28. *Ibid.*, 211:5, 211:10, 228:56; LCWC, 41:12; Chao, "National University," pp. 115–118.

29. HCP, 215:4–16, 237:16.

30. HCP, 220:5; CPPM, 64:1–10.

31. HCP, 220:3; compare CPPM, 63:1–14.

32. Okazaki, "Wang's domestic policy," pp. 186–187; see also CTYL, 130:3.

33. HCP, 219:2.

34. *Ibid.*, 211:14.

35. *Ibid.*, 213:4, 234:13; see also Yang, *Wang*, 2:18.

36. HCP, 248:9, 253:10.

37. Liang, pp. 288–309; K'e, *Wang*, pp. 300–338.

38. LCWC, 42:10–11; Ts'ai, 8:3–4; Liang, pp. 299–300; K'e, *Wang*, pp. 330–331; Williamson, I, 135 and 141, II, 125–126.

39. Ts'ai, 18:7–10; Liang, p. 299; K'e, *Wang*, p. 334; Williamson, II, 125.

40. CPPM, 38:4–9; CTYL, 127:3, 127:8. Wang criticized Fan Chung-yen for seeking fame, for playing politics, and for factionalism; see HCP, 275:11.

41. Ts'ai, 13:6–8; Miyazaki, "Literary class," 159–160.

42. HCP, 210:9–14, 210:18, 211:2–8, 212:1, 213:7–9, 217:2, 219:5–6, 219:10; CPPM, 61:16–19.

43. Ts'ai, 10:10–11, 12:9–10, 19:1; Williamson, II, 128–130.

44. Yang, *Wang*, 1:6; Williamson, I, 175–176; LCWC, 74:21.

45. HCP, 216:13.

46. YYCA, 3:24; Yang, *Wang*, 2:12–13; CPPM, 63:1–14.

47. HCP, 224:1, 224:17–18.

48. *Ibid.*, 253:9.

49. *Ibid.*, chüan, 228–238, *passim*, and especially 240:11 and 245:1.

50. *Ibid.*, 251:16, 259:1–5.

51. On Wang's disagreement with Han Chiang and on Han's dismissal, see HCP, 264:9–11 and 267:11; see also SS, 315:5331–5332. On Wu Ch'ung's failure to support Wang, see HCP, 278:10. Wang, for reasons that are not clear, never waivered in his confidence in Lü Chia-wen who, although criticized by many other officials, was in charge of the controversial State Trade System and Guild Exemption Tax; see HCP, 264:11–12, 268:14; see also Chapter V, Note 52.

52. Ts'ai, 24:4–6.

53. Miyazaki, "Literary class," pp. 154–155; Chao, "Prefectural schools," pp. 308–309.

54. CTYL, 130:9.

55. Yang, *Wang*, 1:33–35; CPPM. 97:1–98:10.

56. Ts'ai, preface, citing Wang Ming-ch'ing, *Yü-chao hsin-chih*. Williamson, II, 225–226, has a translation of the same. Consult also CTYL, 130:10; CPPM, 161:1–102:18.

57. Yang, *Wang*, 1:33–35.

58. Toyama, "Conservatives and progressives"; CPPM, 121:1–122:16.

59. This classification of bureaucrats is based mainly upon the data from CPPM, SS, SSHP (a Sung dynastic history), SSI (a supplement to Sung dynastic history), YYCA, YYTJC (biographies of the antireformers in the Northern Sung), and SYHA (a history of Sung and Yüan schools of learning). Attention is focused upon such leading associates of Wang as Lü Hui-ch'ing, Tseng Pu, Chang Ch'un, Ts'ai Ch'üeh, and Ts'ai Ching. For the locations of biographical information on them, consult Hung, *et al.*

I presented another paper on the classifications of officials in Chinese historiography to the Third Conference on Chinese Thought at Stockbridge, Mass., in September 1957, which will be published in a symposium volume, *Confucianism in Action*, ed. Arthur F. Wright (Stanford University Press, 1959).

60. Liu, "Fan Chung-yen," pp. 126–130.

61. HCP, 221:4.

62. *Ibid.*, 221:20.

63. See Note 59.

64. LCWC, 93:86–88; SS, 472:5677.

65. HCP, 214:17–21, 215:7, 220:11–12, 225:9, 235:3, 238:15–16, 244:11, 246:21, 247:5.

66. *Ibid.*, 237:20, 238:2, 241:10, 242:7. See also Yang, *Wang*, 2:20.

67. See Note 23, and HCP, 252:11, 253:11.

68. CTYL, 130:4, 130:12, 130:28–29. See also TKIL, *passim*.

69. The classification of Tseng Pu as a treacherous official was criticized by the Ch'ing historian Ch'ien Ta-hsin; see his collected works, referred to as CYTC, 28:16. Consult also TKIL, 9:86.

70. Miyazaki, "Literary class," p. 147, considers Ts'ai Ch'üeh in a rather favorable light. This interpretation is somewhat questionable and probably an overevaluation.

CHAPTER V.

The New Policies and Government Operations

1. HCP, 229:17; see also Miyazaki, *Examination system*, pp. 233–234.
2. HCP, 256:9.
3. Miyazaki, "Local clerks," pp. 10–15.
4. HCP, 221:17, 233:3.
5. *Ibid.*, 232:10.
6. Sogabe, *Finance*, pp. 75–79; HCP, 236:12–13.
7. HCP, 212:5, 251:28.
8. Miyazaki, "Clerks in officialdom." See also HCP, 214:26–28, 228:13, 235:25, 242:1, 246:10, 248:21, 265:8–9, 271:19.
9. CPPM, 75:19–21; see also the discussion of this point in Chapter I, Note 4.
10. HCP, 237:8.
11. Sogabe, *Political customs*, p. 42.
12. HCP, 214:26–28.
13. *Ibid.*, 233:20, 248:13–14.
14. Miyazaki, "Clerks in officialdom," pp. 895–904.
15. HCP, 240:5, 251:20–21, 279:6–7.
16. K'e *Wang*, pp. 97–98; CPPM, 68:1–69:19; 110:5–12. Chu Hsi advocated a similar system of farm loans but to be administered by the wealthy and trustworthy leaders of the community instead of by the local government, which meant the clerks.
17. Imahori, "Ausgleichspeicher," pp. 1091–1095.
18. Araki, "Terre carrée," pp. 341–351; Sudō, *Bureaucratic landholdings*, pp. 485–502; CPPM, 73:1–12; 138:1–6.
19. Miyazaki, "Clerks in officialdom," pp. 880–895. See also HCP, 262:24 and 263:1 on tax evasion under the Hired Service System.
20. Shikimori, "State trade," pp. 27–30; CPPM, 72:1–14; 110:12–15.
21. Sogabe, *Finance*, pp. 29–37 and 484–497; Araki, "Terre carrée," pp. 347–357; Miyazaki, "Local clerks," p. 21, especially note 32.
22. The study of the clerical subbureaucracy is included in the

research on local government in the Ch'ing period by Prof. Ch'ü
T'ung-tsu, Center for East Asian Studies, Harvard University.

23. Nieh, "Military power," pp. 97–103; Miyazaki, "Local
government," pp. 109–112; HCP, 265:23.

24. HCP, 223:13; Higashi, "Wang's agrarian system," p. 197;
Imahori, "Ausgleichspeicher," pp. 1104–1166; Sogabe, *Finance*,
pp. 22–55.

25. Kracke, *Civil Service*, pp. 31–38.

26. HCP, 211:17–18, 240:11.

27. *Ibid.*, 210:2, YYCA, 3:25.

28. HCP, 211:3 and 9.

29. *Ibid.*, 214:29, 215:1, 251:10.

30. Kracke, *Civil Service*, pp. 39–41 and Sogabe, *Finance*, pp.
6–7. Reform of civil service titles in the New Policy era caused
the name San-ssu to be dropped. The entire Finance Commission
became the Hu-pu; but neither its functions nor its internal organization changed significantly.

31. Sogabe, *Finance*, p. 16.

32. HCP, 251:18, 257:7.

33. *Ibid.*, 257:7–8.

34. Sogabe, *Finance*, pp. 7–10.

35. Miyazaki, "Literary class," pp. 154–155.

36. Okazaki, "Wang's domestic policy," pp. 184–188.

37. HCP, 213:4, 278:11.

38. *Ibid.*, 229:5, 243:6 and 14; CPPM, 74:1–5.

39. HCP, 248:17.

40. *Ibid.*, 233:14; Araki, "Subjects for examination," pp. 46–48.

41. CTYL, 130:5; Miyazaki, "Student life," p. 100; consult
also CPPM, 93:7–9.

42. Miyazaki, "Student life," pp. 638–645; Chao, "National
University," pp. 184–189.

43. Saeki, "Imperial police," pp. 186–196.

44. HCP, 220:10, 233:15, 235:23–24.

45. *Ibid.*, 215:8, 253:9.

46. *Ibid.*, 213:6, 215:3, 223:15, 266:11.

47. *Ibid.*, 220:5–6, 222:10.

48. Nieh, "Military power," pp. 87–94.

49. Liu, "Fan Chung-yen," pp. 105–108, 122–125; CPPM,
37:23–24.

50. HCP, 210: *passim*, and 263:24.

51. *Ibid.*, 251:15–18, 252:20.

52. *Ibid.*, 252:2, 12–17, 22–24. The State Trade System and the Guild Exemption Tax, after investigation of maladministration and some revisions of rules and regulations, remained in effect. Lü Chia-wen, though relieved of the responsibility for a while, was again put in charge at the insistence of Wang. See *ibid.*, 255:7, 260:8, 261:10, 272:9, 277:15; see also Chapter IV, Note 51.

53. HCP, 256:9, 260:6–8, 265:5, 278:9. Wang was not active during his second term at the court. He complained that the Emperor took his advice only half of the time.

54. TK, pp. 520–521, *passim*; SHY, *Chih-kuan* section, 36:5–15 and 23–27.

55. HCP, 221:1–2, 229:8–9.

56. *Ibid.*, 238:8. Emperor Shen-tsung, after Wang's retirement, dispatched a eunuch, Li Hsien, to direct the military operations in the northwest over the objections of the censors. This set a precedent for the famous case of the eunuch T'ung Kuan, who was the commanding general of expeditionary forces toward the end of the Northern Sung. See HCP, 279:18–21, 280:14–15, 282:4–5, 284:7–9, 285:2–3.

57. *Ibid.*, 236:12, 240:12. See also Saeki, "Imperial police," pp. 170–172.

58. HCP, 236:12, 239:5, 242:1, 251:8–10, 215:21. See also Ch'üan, "Officials and private trade," pp. 207–208.

59. HCP, 239:6–8, 240:4, 245:9; CPPM, 67:13–15.

60. HCP, 229:6–7.

61. *Ibid.*, 242:8–10.

62. *Ibid.*, 231:8, 235:15–18, 239:8, 242:2–3, 244:9.

63. *Ibid.*, 213:2–3, 251:10. See also SSI, 39:7–8.

64. HCP, 231:8–11, 251:15.

65. *Ibid.*, 251:19–20.

66. *Ibid.*, 251:24, 252:2, 5–7, 12–19, 22–24.

67. SS, 242:5160.

68. *Ibid.*, 467:5670, 468:5670; YYCA, 3:40; HCP, 281:5–6.

69. CTYL, 217:5; Yang, *Wang*, 1:36.

70. SS, 243:5161; CPPM, 113:1–10.

71. SS, 471:5676, 242:5160; TKIL, 9:46–47.

72. SS, 467:5670; YYCA, 3:40; SSI, 39:7.
73. SS, 243:5161; TKIL, 8:11–14, 9:64.
74. SS, 244:5162; TKIL, 9:68–69; CTYL, 127:5–6.

CHAPTER VI.

Service for Local Government: A Case Study

1. Sogabe, *Finance*, pp. 89–94; Nieh, "Local government service," p. 220.
2. Nieh, "Local government service," pp. 197–201.
3. *Ibid.*, pp. 195–197; Kawakami, "Village officials," pp. 61–72.
4. Nieh, "Local government service," pp. 195–197.
5. Sogabe, *Finance*, pp. 108–116.
6. *Ibid.*, pp. 126–128; Miyazaki, "Local clerks," p. 20.
7. Sogabe, *Finance*, p. 141.
8. *Ibid.*, pp. 120–121; Nieh, "Local government service," pp. 214–216. Similar efforts to consolidate the units of local government, after the example of Fan Chung-yen, are usually recorded at the end of each year in HCP.
9. Nieh, "Local government service," pp. 213–214; Sogabe, *Finance*, p. 147–148; Williamson, I, 219–222.
10. Nieh, "Local government service," pp. 223–224; Sogabe, *Finance*, pp. 147–148; Williamson, I, 222–225.
11. Nieh, "Local government service," pp. 224–225; Sogabe, *Finance*, pp. 150–161; CPPM, 70:1–15.
12. HCP, 257:8, 263:17.
13. TK, 12:132–133; HCP, 245:16–17, 277:12.
14. Nieh, "Local government service," pp. 226–237; Sogabe, *Finance*, pp. 162–169. For the most outspoken objections raised by Yang Hui and Liu Chih, see HCP, 223:5–6, 223:12–14, 224:3–5, 7–9, and 15–17.
15. HCP, 215:7, 225:2–17.
16. *Ibid.*, 234:4.
17. *Ibid.*, 237:19.
18. *Ibid.*, 223:16–17.
19. *Ibid.*, 279:18; Sogabe, *Finance*, pp. 153–161.

20. Sogabe, *Finance*, pp. 186–191; Nieh, "Local government service," pp. 240–247; CPPM, 108:1–23.

21. Sogabe, *Finance*, pp. 191–244; Nieh, "Local government service," pp. 255–268.

22. Sogabe, *Finance*, pp. 181–182.

23. HCP, 220:15 and *chüan* 223–225, *passim*.

24. *Ibid.*, 223:11, 242:1.

25. *Ibid.*, 217:11–13, 246:9; Sogabe, *Finance*, pp. 186–191.

26. Yang, *Money and Credit*, pp. 37–38, 44–45.

27. Ch'üan, "Price fluctuations," pp. 389–391.

28. Sogabe, *Finance*, pp. 173 and 189; Nieh, "Local government service," pp. 245–246.

29. HCP, 239:4.

30. *Ibid.*, 267:6; Sogabe, *Finance*, pp. 199 ff.

31. Nieh, "Local government service," pp. 251–270.

Index

REFERENCE MATTER

Bibliography
Glossary

BIBLIOGRAPHY

Almost all the works by Chinese and Japanese scholars listed below are in their own language respectively.

Aoyama Sadao 青山定雄. "The New Bureaucrats and Kiangsi Regions during the Five Dynasties and the Sung," Wada Hakushi kanreki kinen Tōyōshi ronsō 和田博士還曆紀念 東洋史論叢 (Asiatic studies in honor of Dr. Wada Sei 和田清), pp. 19-37. Tokyo: Dai-Nippon Yūbenkai Kōdansha 大日本雄辯會講談社, 1951.

Araki Toshikazu 荒木敏一. "La prohibition de cuivre et la levée de cette interdiction par Wang An-chi (Wang An-shih)," Tōyōshi kenkyū 東洋史研究, 4:1-29 (Kyoto, 1938).

------- "Le système d'imposition égalitaire au moyen de la 'terre carrée' sous les Soung," Tōyōshi kenkyū, 6:331-351 (Kyoto, 1941).

------- "Subjects for Examinations Held in the Palace during the Sung Dynasty," Tōyōshi ronsō: Haneda Hakushi shōju kinen 東洋史論叢: 羽田博士頌壽紀念 (Asiatic studies in honor of Dr. Haneda Tōru 羽田亨), pp. 37-48. Tokyo: Tōyōshi Kenkyūkai 東洋史研究會, 1950.

CCTSC: Ch'ao Kung-wu 晁公武. Chün-chai tu-shu chih 郡齋讀書志 (Ch'ao's bibliographical notes). Ssu-pu ts'ung-k'an 四部叢刊 ed.; Shanghai: Commercial Press, 1929.

Ch'ai Te-keng 柴德賡. "On the Participation of the Sung Eunuchs in Military Affairs," Fu-jen hsüeh-chih 輔仁學誌, 10:181-225 (Peking, 1941).

Chang Chia-chü 張家駒. "The Society in Southern China Shortly before the Southern Sung," Shih-huo 食貨, 4:28-41 (Peking, 1936).

i

Chao I 趙翼. Nien-erh-shih cha-chi 廿二史劄記 (Notes on the twenty-two histories). Shih-chieh Shu-chü 世界書局 ed.; Shanghai, 1936.

Chao T'ieh-han 趙鐵寒. "The National University of the Sung Dynasty," Ta-lu 大陸, 7:115-118, 150-155, 184-189 (Taipeh, 1953).

------- "The Prefectural Schools of the Sung Dynasty," Ta-lu, 7:305-309, 341-343 (Taipeh, 1953).

Ch'ao Kung-wu, see CCTSC.

Ch'en Chen-sun, see SMCT.

Ch'en Chung-fan 陳鐘凡. Liang Sung ssu-hsiang shu-p'ing 兩宋思想述評 (An analysis of Sung thought). Shanghai: Commercial Press, 1933.

Ch'en K'u, see HTC.

Chiang Hao 姜豪. Wang An-shih hsin-cheng kang-yao 王安石新政綱要 (The principles of Wang An-shih's New Policies). Shanghai: Kuo-min T'u-shu Hu-chu-hui 國民圖書互助會, 1935.

Ch'ien Mu 錢穆. Sung Ming li-hsüeh kai-shu 宋明理學概述 (An outline of Neo-Confucianism in the Sung and Ming periods). Taipeh: Chung-hua Wen-hua Ch'u-pan Shih-yeh Wei-yüan-hui 中華文化出版事業委員會, 1953.

Ch'ien Ta-hsin, see CYTC.

Chou Ming-t'ai 周明泰. San Tseng nien-p'u 三曾年譜 (An annalistic biography of the three Tseng brothers). Peking, 1932.

Chu Hsi, see CTYL and MCYHL.

Chü Ch'ing-yüan 鞠清遠. "The Southern Sung Officials and Trade and Industries," Shih-huo, 2:367-375 (Peking, 1935).

Ch'ü T'ung-tsu 瞿同祖 . Chung-kuo fa-lü yü Chung-kuo she-hui 中國法律與中國社會 (Chinese law and Chinese society). Shanghai: Commercial Press, 1947.

Ch'üan Han-sheng 全漢昇 . "Government Officials and Private Trade in the Sung Dynasty," Bulletin of the Institute of History and Philology, Academia Sinica, 7:199-254 (Nanking, 1936).

------- "Export and Import Trade of the East Capital of the Northern Sung Dynasty," Bulletin of the Institute of History and Philology, Academia Sinica, 8.2:189-306 (Chungking, 1939).

------- "Price Fluctuations during the Northern Sung Period," Bulletin of the Institute of History and Philology, Academia Sinica, 11:337-394 (Nanking, 1947).

------- "Natural Economy in the Medieval Ages of China," Bulletin of the Institute of History and Philology, Academia Sinica, 10:73-173 (Nanking, 1948).

------- "The Relation between the Public Revenue and Money Economy during the T'ang and the Sung Periods," Bulletin of the Institute of History and Philology, Academia Sinica, 20:189-224 (Nanking, 1948).

CKHI: Wang An-shih 王安石 . Chou-kuan hsin-i 周官新義 (A new interpretation of the Chou institutions); in Yüeh-ya-t'ang ts'ung-shu 粵雅堂叢書 . N.p., ca. 1850.

CPPM: Yang Chung-liang 楊仲良 . T'ung-chien ch'ang-pien chi-shih pen-mo 通鑑長編紀事本末 (A topical re-arrangement of the HCP). Shanghai: Kuang-ya Shu-chü 廣雅書局 , 1893.

CTYL: Chu Hsi 朱熹 . Chu-tzu yü-lei 朱子語類 (The classified comments of Chu Hsi). Ch'uan-ching-t'ang 傳經堂 ed.; n.p., 1876.

CYCSC: Yüan Chüeh 袁桷 . Ch'ing-yung-chü-shih chi 清容居士集 (The collected works of Yüan Chüeh). Ssu-pu-pei-yao 四部備要 ed.; Shanghai, 1936.

CYTC: Ch'ien Ta-hsin 錢大昕 . Ch'ien-yen-t'ang chi 潛研堂集 (The collected works of Ch'ien). Ssu-pu-ts'ung-k'an ed.; Shanghai: Commercial Press, 1929.

CYYL: Li Hsin-ch'uan 李心傳 . Chien-yen i-lai hsi-nien yao-lu 建炎以來繫年要錄 (An annual history since the beginning of the Southern Sung). Chung-hua Shu-chü 中華書局 reprint of the Commercial Press ed.; Shanghai, 1956.

de Bary, Wm. Theodore. "A Reappraisal of Neo-Confucianism, " Studies in Chinese Thought, ed. Arthur F. Wright. Chicago: University of Chicago Press, 1953.

Ferguson, John C. "Wang An-shih,"Journal of North China Branch of the Royal Asiatic Society, 35: 65-75 (Shanghai, 1903-1904).

Fischer, J. "Fan Chung-yen (989-1052). Das Lebensbild eines Chinesischen Staats-mannes, " Oriens Extremus, 2: 39-85, 142-156 (Hamburg, 1955).

HCP: Li T'ao 李燾 . Hsü tzu-chih-t'ung-chien ch'ang-pien 續資治通鑑長編 (A collection of materials for an annalistic history of the Northern Sung). Hangchow: Chekiang Shu-chü 浙江書局 , 1881.

Higashi Kazuo 東一夫 . "A Study of Wang An-shih's Agrarian System with Reference to Local Peculiarities, " Tōyō shiga-ku ronshū 東洋史學論叢, 2: 189-204 (Tokyo, 1953).

------- "Land survey and tax": "A Study of the Character of Fang-t'ien chun-shui fa , " Tōyō shigaku ronshū, 3: 227-290 (Tokyo, 1954).

Hino, K. 日野開三郎. "Über die Prägungssumme der Kupfer und Eisenmünzen im prae-Sung Zeitalter," Shigaku zasshi 史學雜誌, 46:46-105 (Tokyo, 1935).

Ho Yu-shen 何佑森. "The Geographic Distribution of Sung Scholarship," Hsin-ya 新亞, 1:331-339 (Hongkong, 1955).

Hsia Chün-yü 夏君虞. Sung-hsüeh kai-yao 宋學概要 (An outline of Sung learning). Shanghai: Commercial Press, 1937.

Hsiao Kung-ch'üan 蕭公權. Chung-kuo cheng-chih ssu-hsiang shih 中國政治思想史 (A history of Chinese political thought). Vol. 2; Shanghai: Commercial Press, 1946.

Hsiung Kung-che 熊公哲. Wang An-shih cheng-lüeh 王安石政略 (An outline of Wang An-shih's policy). Shanghai: Commercial Press, 1937.

HTC: Ch'en K'u 陳鵠. Hsi-t'ang-chi ch'i-chiu-hsü-wen 西塘集耆舊續聞 (Information gathered from the elders); in Chih-pu-tsu-chai ts'ung-shu 知不足齋叢書. Shanghai: Ku-shu Liu-t'ung-ch'u 古書流通處, 1921.

HTK: Hsü wen-hsien t'ung-k'ao 續文獻通考 (The supplement to the encyclopedia Wen-hsien t'ung-k'ao). See TK.

Hu Yun-i 胡雲翼. Sung-shih yen-chiu 宋詩研究 (A study of Sung poetry). Shanghai: Commercial Press, 1930.

Huang Tsung-hsi, see SYHA.

Hung, William 洪業, Nieh Ch'ung-ch'i 聶崇岐, et al., eds. Ssu-shih-ch'i chung Sung-tai chuang-chi tsung-ho yin-te 四十七種宋代傳記綜合引得 (Combined indices to forty-seven collections of Sung dynasty biographies). Peking: Harvard-Yenching Institute, 1939.

Ikeda Mabota 池田誠, "Tithing system": "Origin and Development of the Tithing System," Tōyōshi kenkyū, 12:481-512 (Kyoto, 1954).

Imahori Senji 今堀誠二 . "Eine Untersuchung über die 'Ausgleich-speicher' in der Sung Zeit," Shigaku zasshi, 56:959-1028, 1055-1111 (Tokyo, 1946).

Katō Shigeru 加藤繁 . "On the Commercial Taxes of the Sung Dynasty," Shirin 史林 , 19:604-652 (Kyoto, 1934).

------- "Silver Currency and Its Relations with Hui-tzu during the Southern Sung Dynasty," Tōyō gakuhō 東洋學報 , 14:560-614 (Tokyo, 1944).

Kawakami Koichi 河上光一 , "Village officials": "On the Li-cheng, Hu-chang, and Ch'i-chang during the Sung Dynasty," Tōyō gakuhō, 14:61-76 (Tokyo, 1952).

KCWC: Ou-yang Hsüan 歐陽玄 . Kwei-chai wen-chi 圭齋文集 (The collected works of Ou-yang Hsüan). Ssu-pu-ts'ung-k'an ed.; Shanghai: Commercial Press, 1929.

K'e Ch'ang-i 柯昌頤 . Wang An-shih p'ing-chuan 王安石評傳 (A critical biography of Wang An-shih). Shanghai: Commercial Press, 1933.

K'e Tun-po 柯敦伯 . Sung wen-hsüeh shih 宋文學史 (A history of Sung literature). Shanghai: Commercial Press, 1934.

K'e Wei-ch'i, see SSHP.

Kracke, E. A., Jr. Civil Service in Early Sung China 960-1067. Cambridge, Mass.: Harvard University Press, 1953.

------- "Sung Society: Change within Tradition," Far Eastern Quarterly, 14:479-488 (1955).

------- Civil Service Titles. Paris: Sung Project, École Pratique des Hautes Études, 1957.

Kuo Shao-yü 郭紹虞 . Sung shih-hua chi-i 宋詩話輯佚 (Fragments of Sung criticism of poetry). Peking: Harvard-Yenching Institute, 1937.

LCCSI: Wang An-shih. Lin-ch'uan-chi shih-i 臨川集拾遺 (A supplement to the collected works of Wang An-shih). Shanghai: Chü-chen-fang-Sung Shu-chü 聚珍仿宋書局, 1918.

LCWC: Wang An-shih. Lin-ch'uan wen-chi 臨川文集 (The collected works of Wang An-shih). Wan-yu-wen-k'u 萬有文庫 ed.; Shanghai: Commercial Press, 1933.

Li Hsin-chuan, see CYYL.

Li T'ao, see HCP.

Li Wen-chih 李文治. "The Economic Force behind the People's Rebellions in the Northern Sung Period," Shih-ho, 4:464-484 (Peking, 1936).

Liang Ch'i-ch'ao 梁啟超. Wang Ching-kung chuan 王荊公傳 (Biography of Wang An-shih); in Yin-ping-shih ts'ung-shu 飲冰室叢書. Shanghai: Commercial Press, 1917.

Lin Yutang. The Gay Genius, the Life and Times of Su Tungpo. New York: John Day Co., 1947.

Liu, James T.C. (Liu Tzu-chien 劉子健). "An Early Sung Reformer: Fan Chung-yen," Chinese Thought and Institutions, ed. John K. Fairbank. Chicago: University of Chicago Press, 1957.

------- "Mei Yao-ch'en" 梅堯臣, occasional paper of the Sung Project, SP/II.1/12.12.56:1-9 (Paris, 1956).

------- "Fan Chung-yen, Mei Yao-chen, and the Political Struggle of the Northern Sung," Tōhōgaku 東方學, 14:104-107 (Tokyo, 1957).

Lu Hsin-yüan, see SSI and YYTJC.

Ma Tuan-lin, see TK.

MCYHL: Chu Hsi. Ming-ch'en yen-hsing lu 名臣言行錄 (The words and conduct of the famous officials). Ssu-pu-ts'ung-k'an ed.; Shanghai: Commercial Press, 1929.

Miyazaki Ichisada 宮崎市定. "Student Life under the Sung Dynasty," Shirin, 16:97-105, 625-651 (Kyoto, 1931).

------- "Wang An-shih's Policy to Include the Clerks in Officialdom," Kuwabara Hakushi kinen Tōyōshi ronsō 桑原博士紀念 東洋史論叢 (Asiatic studies in honor of Dr. Kuwabara), pp. 859-904. Kyoto: Kōbundo, 1931.

------- "Luxury": "Zum Chinesischen Luxus -- ein Beitrag zur Abwechslung des Luxes in China," Shigaku zasshi, 51:27-56 (Tokyo, 1940).

------- "Courte biographie de Tchia Shi-tao (Chia Ssu-tao)," Tōyōshi kenkyū, 6:218-237 (Kyoto, 1941).

------- Godai Sō chō nō tsūka mondai 五代宋初の通貨問題 (The currency problem during the Five Dynasties and early Sung). Kyoto: Hoshino Shoten 星野書店, 1943.

------- "Local clerks": "On the Question of Local Government Clerks," Shirin, 30:1-27 (Kyoto, 1945).

------- Kakyo 科擧 (The examination system). Ōsaka: Akidaya 秋田屋, 1946.

------- "The Morals of the Literary Class in the Sung Period," Shigaku zasshi, 62:139-169 (Tokyo, 1953).

------- "Local government": "The Chou-hsien System under the Sung Dynasty -- an Essay on the History of the Ya-ch'ien," Shirin, 36:101-127 (Kyoto, 1953).

Morohashi Tetsuji 諸橋轍次. "The Key Position of Li T'ao-po (Li Kou) in Confucian History," Shibun 斯文, 8:445-467 (Tokyo, 1926).

------- Sung Confucianists: Jugaku no mokuteki to Sō-ju 儒學の 目的と宋儒 (The purposes of Confucian learning and the Sung Confucianists).　Tokyo: Taishukan 大修館, 1930.

------- Jukyō no sho mondai 儒教の諸問題 (The various problems of Confucianism).　Tokyo: Shimizu Shoten 清水書店, 1948.

Mou Jun-sun 牟潤孫.　"The Main Stream of the Ch'un-ch'iu Study during the Sung," Ta-lu, 5:113-117, 170-172 (Taipeh, 1952).

Nagase Mamoru 長瀨守.　"The Land Policy of the New Institutional Party during the Period of Hsi-ning in the Northern Sung Dynasty," Tōyō shigaku ronshū, 3:239-252 (Tokyo, 1954).

Naitō Torajirō 内藤虎次郎.　Chūgoku kinsei shi 中國近世史 (A history of modern China).　Tokyo: Kōbundo 弘文堂, 1947.

Nakamura, G. 中村治兵衛.　"The Coming to Power of Wang An-shih," Rekishi-gaku kenkyū 歷史學研究, 157:1-12 (Tokyo, 1952).

Nieh Ch'ung-ch'i, "Local government service": "The Yi-fa or I-fa of the Sung Dynasty," Yenching hsüeh-pao 燕京學報, 33:195-270 (Peking, 1947).

------- "Discussion of Sung T'ai-tsu's Resumption of Military Power," Yenching hsüeh-pao, 34:85-106 (Peking, 1948).

Nishi Junzō 西順藏.　"On the Thoughts of Three Literati in the North Sung Dynasty," The Hitotsubashi Review 一橋論叢, 26:30-52 (Tokyo, 1951).

Ogasawara Shōji 小笠原正治, "Archers": "Character and Organization of the Kung-chien-shou in the Sung Dynasty," Tōyō shigakū ronshū, 3:81-94 (Tokyo, 1954).

Okazaki Fukio 岡崎丈夫.　"Wang An-shih's Domestic Policy," Shinagaku 支那學, 9:173-188 (Kyoto, 1938).

Ou-yang Hsüan, see KCWC.

P'an Yung-ku, see SPLC.

Saeki Tomi 佐伯富. "On Huang-ch'eng-ssu or the Imperial Court
    Police Service," Tōhō gakuhō, 9:158-196 (Kyoto, 1938).

------- Wang An-shih. Tokyo: Fujibo 富士房 , 1941.

------- "The 'Heavy Penalty Places' in the Sung Period," Tōyōshi
    ronsō: Haneda Hakushi shōju kinen (Asiatic studies in honor
    of Dr. Haneda Tōru), pp. 505-530. Tokyo: Tōyōshi Kenkyū-
    kai, 1950.

Shikimori Tomiji 式守富司 , "State trade": "Shih-i-fa of Wang An-
    shih," Rekishi-gaku kenkyū, 6:2-30 (Tokyo, 1936).

SHY: Sung hui-yao chi-kao 宋會要輯稿 (Collected draft of
    classified information on the government institutions during
    the Sung dynasty). Re-collected by Hsü Sung from the en-
    cyclopedia Yung-lo ta-tien; Peking: the National Library of
    Peking, 1936.

SJIS: Ting Ch'uan-ching 丁傳靖 , compiler. Sung-jen i-shih hui-
    pien 宋人軼事彙編 (Anthology of Sung anecdotes).
    Shanghai: Commercial Press, 1935.

SMCT: Ch'en Chen-sun 陳振孫. Chih-chai shu-lu chieh-t'i 直
    齋書錄解題 (Ch'en's bibliographical guide). Shanghai:
    Kiangsu Shu-chü 江蘇書局 , 1883.

Sogabe Shizuo 曾吾部靜雄. Sō dai zaisei shi 宋代財政史
    (A history of Sung dynasty finance). Tokyo: Seikatsusha 生
    活社 , 1941.

------- Shina seiji shūzoku ronkō 支那政治習俗論考 (On
    Chinese political customs). Tokyo: Tsukuma Shobo, 1943.

SPLC: P'an Yung-yin 潘永因 , compiler. Sung pei lei-ch'ao 宋

裨類鈔 (A topical anthology of Sung anecdotes). N. p. , 1669.

SS: T'o-t'o 脫脫 et al. , ed. Sung-shih 宋史 (Sung dynastic history). Twenty-five Dynastic Histories ed.; Shanghai: K'ai-ming Shu-tien 開明書店 , 1934.

SSHP: K'e Wei-ch'i 柯維騏. Sung-shih hsin-pien 宋史新編 (A new Sung dynastic history). N. p. , 1557.

SSI: Lu Hsin-yüan 陸心源. Sung-shih i 宋史翼 (A supplement to Sung dynastic history). Kueian, 1906.

Sudō Yoshiyuki 周藤吉之 . Sō dai kanryōshi to daitochi shoyū 宋代官僚系 と 大土地所有 (The Sung bureaucratic system and large landholdings). Vol. 8 of Shakai kōseishi taikei 社會構成史體系 ; Tokyo: Nippon Hyōronsha 日本評論所 , 1950.

------- Chūgoku tochi seidoshi kenkyū 中國土地制度史研究 (A study in the history of the Chinese land system). Tokyo: Tōyō-bunka Kenkyū-jo 東洋文庫研究社 , 1954.

Sung hui-yao chi-kao, see SHY.

Sung Lien, see YS.

Suzuki, C. 鈴木中正 , "Sung buddhism": "Über die Gesellschaft für Buddhismus im Zeitalter der Sung-dynastie, " Shigaku Zasshi, 52:65-98 (Tokyo, 1941).

SYHA: Huang Tsung-hsi 黃宗義 . Sung Yüan hsüeh-an 宋元學案 (A history of Sung and Yüan schools of learning). Shanghai: Shih-chieh Shu-chü, 1936.

Takeuchi Yoshio 武内義雄 . "The Origins and the Characteristics of Sung Learning, " Tōyō Shichō 東洋思潮 , 11:1-50 (Tokyo, 1934).

T'ao Hsi-sheng 陶希聖 . "The Unfair Burden and the Reform of

the Land Tax before Wang An-shih, " Shih-huo, 1:20-22 (Peking, 1934).

------- "The Economic and Financial Problems in the Early Sung, " Shih-huo, 2:83-90 (Peking, 1935).

------- "The Office Land during the Sung Dynasty, " Shih-huo, 2: 195-197 (Peking, 1935).

------- "The Well-field Theory of the Great Thinkers in the Northern Sung, " Shih-huo, 2:281-284 (Peking, 1935).

Teng Kuang-ming 鄧廣銘 , "Government officials": "Commentary on the 'Chih-kuan-chih' of Sung dynastic history, " Bulletin of the Institute of History and Philology, Academia Sinica, 10: 433-593 (Nanking, 1948).

------- Wang An-shih. Peking: San-lien Shu-tien, 1953.

Ting Ch'uan-ching, see SJIS.

TK: Ma Tuan-lin 馬端臨 . Wen-hsien t'ung-k'ao 文獻通考 (An encyclopedia of historical institutions). Wan-yu-wen-k'u ed.; Shanghai: Commercial Press, 1936.

TKIL: Tseng Pu 曾布 . Tseng-kung i-lu 曾公遺錄 (Notes of Tseng Pu); Ou-hsiang ling-shih 藕香零拾 collection, chüan 22-24. N.p., 1910.

T'o-t'o, see SS.

Toyama Gunji 外山軍治 . "Antagonism between the Conservatives and the Progressives at the Time of the Downfall of the Northern Sung in 1126, " Tōyōshi ronsō: Haneda Hakushi shojū kinen (Asiatic studies in honor of Dr. Haneda Tōru), pp. 663-668. Tokyo: Tōyōshi Kenkyūkai, 1950.

Ts'ai Shang-hsiang 蔡上翔 . Wang Ching-kung nien-p'u k'ao-lüeh 王荊公年譜考略 (An annalistic biography of Wang An-

shih and its research evidence). Peking: Harvard-Yenching
Institute, 1930.

Tseng Pu, see TKIL.

Tu Ta-kuei, see YYCA.

Wang An-shih, see CKHI, LCCSI, and LCWC.

Wang Chih-jui 王志瑞 . Sung Yüan ching-chi shih
(An economic history of the Sung and the Yüan). Shanghai:
Commercial Press, 1931.

Wang Hsin-jui 王興瑞 . "Wang An-shih's Reform and Irrigation
Policy, " Shih-huo, 2:91-95 (Peking, 1935).

Wang Yü-ch'üan 王毓銓 . "The Northern Sung Society, Economy,
and Politics -- a Preface to Wang An-shih's Reform, " Shih-
huo, 3:535-546, 577-598 (Peking, 1936).

Williamson, H.R. Wang An-shih, Chinese Statesman and Education-
alist of the Sung Dynasty. 2 vols.; London: A. Probsthain,
1935-1937.

Wright, Arthur F. "Buddhism and Chinese Culture: Phases of Inter-
action, " The Journal of Asian Studies, 17:17-42 (1957).

Yang Chung-liang, see CPPM.

Yang Hsi-min 楊希閔 . Wang Ching-kung nien-p'u k'ao-lüeh fu-
ts'un 王荊公年譜考略附存 (Supplementary evi-
dence to the annalistic biography of Wang An-shih). Last
volume of Ts'ai Shang-hsiang, Wang Ching-kung nien-p'u
k'ao-lüeh.

Yang Lien-sheng 楊聯陞 . Money and Credit in China. Cambridge,
Mass.: Harvard University Press, 1951.

Yoshida Tora 吉田寅 . "A Study of the Discussions on Tax on Salt
in Hopei in the Northern Sung Dynasty, " Tōyō shigaku ronshū,
3:409-422 (Tokyo, 1954).

YS: Sung Lien 宋濂 , ed. Yüan-shih 元史 (Yüan dynastic history).
Twenty-five Dynastic Histories ed.; Shanghai: K'ai-ming Shu-
tien, 1934.

Yüan Chüeh, see CYCSC.

YYCA: Tu Ta-kuei 杜大珪 . Yüan-yen-chi shan-ts'un 琬琰集
冊存 (An abridged collection of early Sung biographies).
Peking: Harvard-Yenching Institute, 1938.

YYTJC: Lu Hsin-yüan. Yüan-yu tang-jen chuan 元祐黨人傳
(Biographies of the anti-reformers in the Northern Sung).
N. p. , 1889.

Aoyama Sadao 青山定雄

Ch'ai-i-fa 差役法

Ch'an (or Zen) 禪

Chang Ch'un 章淳

Chang Fang-p'ing 張方平

Chang River 漳河

Chang-ssu 帳司

ch'ang 場

Ch'ang Chih 常秩

Ch'ang-chou 常州

ch'ang ming ya-ch'ien 長名衙前

Ch'ang-p'ing-ssu 常平司

ch'ang-p'ing-ts'ang 常平倉

ch'ang yü li-shih 長於吏事

Chao-tz'u 昭慈

Che-tsung 哲宗

Chen-hsien 鄞縣

Chen-tsung 真宗

Ch'en Yen 陳衍

cheng 政

Cheng Hsia 鄭俠

cheng-ming 正名

ch'eng-fu 承符

Chi-hsien Library 集賢閣

ch'i-chang 耆長

chia 甲

ch'ia-tzu 掐子

chiang-li ya ch'ien 將吏衙前

chiao 教

chieh 誡

chieh-tzu 解子

ch'ien 錢

Chien-ch'en chüan 姦臣傳

Chien-chung 建中

ch'ien-huang 錢荒

Chih-chih-kao 知制誥

Chih-chih San-ssu T'iao-li Ssu 制置三司條例司

chih-i 職役

ch'ih 恥

chin 津

chin-shih 進士

chin-tu 津渡

ching-i 經義

ching-lun 經綸

ch'ing 情

Ch'ing-miao Ch'ien 青苗錢

ch'ing wang kuan 清望官

Chou-hsüeh 州學

Chou-li 周禮

Chou Tun-i 周敦頤

Chu Hsi 朱熹

chuan-yün-ssu 轉運司

chuang-ting 壯丁

Ch'un-ch'iu 春秋

chung 忠

chung-shu men-hsia 中書門下

chü 舉

Ch'ü T'ung-tsu 瞿同祖

Ch'üan-chou (or Zayton) 泉州

Ch'üan Han-sheng 全漢昇

Chün-ch'i-chien 軍器監

Chün-shu 均輸

chün-tzu 君子

fa 法

fa-chih 法制

fa-tu 法度

Fan Ch'un-jen 范純仁

Fan Chung-yen 范仲淹

fang 坊

Fang-t'ien Chün-shui 方田均稅

Farming Loans, see Ch'ing-miao
　　　Ch'ien

feng-chien 封建

Feng Ching 馮京

feng-su 風俗

fu 賦

Fu-chou 撫州

fu-kuo ch'iang-ping 富國強兵

Fu Pi 富弼

Han Chiang 韓絳

Han Ch'i 韓琦

Han-fei-tzu 韓非子

Han Wei 韓維

hsiang-hu ya-ch'ien 鄉戶衙前

hsiang-kuan 鄉官

hsiang-shu-shou 鄉書手

hsiao-jen 小人

Hsiao Kung-ch'üan 蕭公權

Hsieh Ching-wen 謝景文

hsin 信

hsin-fa 新法

Hsin Hsüeh 新學

hsing 刑

hsing 性

Hsü tzu-chih-t'ung-chien ch'ang-
　　　pien 續資治通鑑長
　　編

Hsüan-jen 宣仁

Hsüeh Hsiang 薛向

hsün-li 循吏

Hsün-tzu 荀子

hu-chang 戶長

Hu-pu 戶部

Hu Yüan 胡瑗

Huang-ch'eng-ssu 皇城司

Hui-tsung 徽宗

i 義

i 役

I-ching 易經

i-fa 役法

jen 仁

jen 任

jen-li 人力

Jen-tsung 仁宗

K'ai-feng 開封

kan-ts'ai 幹才

kao 誥

Kao-tsung 高宗

K'e Ch'ang-i 柯昌頤

k'e-ssu 客司

Kiang-ning 江寧

k'u-tzu 庫子

K'uai-chi-ssu 會計司

k'uan-sheng-ch'ien 寬剩錢

kung-chien-shou 弓箭手

kung-shou 弓手

li 禮

li 利

li-cheng 里正

li-cheng ya-ch'ien 里正衙前

li-i 隸役

Li Kou 李覯

Li T'ao 李燾

Li Ting 李定

Liang Ch'i-ch'ao 梁啟超

liang-li 良吏

liang-shui-fa 兩稅法

lien 廉

Lin-ch'uan 臨川

ling 令

Liu Chih 劉摯

liu-min-t'u 流民圖

Liu Yen 劉晏

Lo 洛

Loyang 洛陽

lun 論

Lü Hui-ch'ing 呂惠卿

Lü Kung-chu 呂公著

Lü Ta-fang 呂大防

Lü T'ao 呂陶

men-hsia-k'e 門下客

mien-hang-ch'ien 免行錢

mien-i-ch'ien 免役錢

Miyazaki Ichisada 宮崎市定

Mu-i Fa 募役法

Naitō Torajirō 内藤虎次郎

Nan-ching 難經

neng-li 能吏

Nieh Ch'ung-ch'i 聶崇岐

nung-ch'üan 弄權

Ou-yang Hsiu 歐陽修

pa 霸

Pao-chia 保甲

Pao-jen 保任

Pao-ma Fa 保馬法

Pen-ts'ao 本草
pi-chi 筆記
"Pien chien lun" 辯姦論
Pien River 汴河
P'u 濮

shan-ch'üan 擅權
shan li-shih 善吏事
Sang Hung-yang 桑弘羊
San-ssu 三司
san-ts'ung 散從
Shang Yang 商鞅
Shao Yung 邵雍
shen-ming 神明
Shen-tsung 神宗
shih 詩
Shih-i Fa 市易法
Shih-lu 實錄
shou-li 手力
Shu 蜀
shu 術
Shu-kuo, Duke of 舒國公
Shu-mi-yüan 樞密院
shu-piao-ssu 書裱司
Shuo 朔
Sogabe Shizuo 曽我部静雄
Ssu-ma Kuang 司馬光
Ssu-nung-shih 司農寺
Ssu-t'ien-chien 司天監
Su Ch'e 蘇轍

Su-chou 宿州
Su Hsün 蘇洵
Su Shih 蘇軾
Su-wen 素問
Sudō Yoshiyuki 周藤吉之
Sun Fu 孫復
Sung hui-yao chi-kao 宋會要輯稿
Sung-shih 宋史

T'ai-hsüeh 太學
t'an-kuan 貪官
tang 黨
Teng Chien 鄧縮
tien-li 典吏
t'ing-tzu 廷子
tou-tzu 斗子
tsai-hsiang 宰相
Ts'ai Ching 蔡京
Ts'ai Ch'üeh 蔡確
Ts'ai Pien 蔡卞
Ts'ai Shang-hsiang 蔡上翔
ts'an-chih-cheng-shih 參知政事
Ts'ang fa 倉法
ts'e 策
Tseng Pu 曾布
ts'ui-shui chia-t'ou 催稅甲頭
Tu-chih 度支
t'ung chung-shu men-hsia p'ing-chang shih 同中書門下平章事

HARVARD EAST ASIAN SERIES